FULL CIRCLE

The Remarkable True Story of Two All-American
Wrestling Teammates Pitted Against Each Other in
the War on Drugs and Then Reunited as Coaches

CHUCK MALKUS

WITH

JERRY LANGTON

Skyhorse Publishing

Skyhorse Publishing books may be purchased in bulk at special discounts for sales promotion, corporate gifts, fund-raising, or educational purposes. Special editions can also be created to specifications. For details, contact the Special Sales Department, Skyhorse Publishing, 307 West 36th Street, 11th Floor, New York, NY 10018 or info@skyhorsepublishing.com.

Skyhorse® and Skyhorse Publishing® is are registered trademarks of Skyhorse Publishing, Inc.®, a Delaware corporation.
 Visit our website at www.skyhorsepublishing.com.

10 9 8 7 6 5 4 3 2 1

Library of Congress Cataloging-in-Publication Data is available on file.

Cover design by Tom Lau
Front cover photos: Barry Zimler (top left and right), James Burke, Boca Raton Police Department (bottom left), Patrick Farrell, From the Miami Herald, April 6, 1997 © 1997 McClatchy. All rights reserved. Used by permission and protected by the Copyright Laws of the United States. (bottom right)

Back cover photo: Sandra Padilla Malkus, From Malkus Group, © 2017. All rights reserved.

Print ISBN: 978-1-5107-2466-2
Ebook ISBN: 978-1-5107-2468-6

Printed in the United States of America

CONTENTS

Acknowledgments

Two All-American teammates who ended up on opposing sides of the law is a story that has spanned four decades. I'll always remember when I first witnessed Kevin Pedersen and Alex DeCubas on the wrestling mat as juniors at Palmetto High School. I was a sports correspondent for *The Miami News*, a high school student myself, at another school.

There was something very unique about these two guys and it was more than the differences in their height and weight. Kevin was quiet, getting it done through hard work and a special dedication to practice. His teammate, Alex, well, he simply achieved success with God-given abilities.

They both earned titles as state champions, their photos appearing in *Sports Illustrated*. One of the stories I wrote was the selection by Pedersen to attend West Point Academy and Alex's choice of the University of Georgia.

When I began my first career position as a sports editor at the daily *South Dade News Leader*, there was a reason to avoid Alex DeCubas. He had become a cocaine cowboy and someone who was known to throw his coke earnings around Miami like money was going out of style. Meanwhile, Kevin Pedersen was one of many friends on the other side of America's cocaine madness in the 1980s through the 1990s. As a DEA agent, Pedersen was one of the good guys in the shadows trying to clean up the messy War on Drugs.

The size and magnitude of this story has required assembling a team to help conduct research from several cities in the United States in addition to the countries of Colombia, Brazil, and England. I'm grateful for my co-writer Jerry Langton, who went the extra mile in researching and connecting this story. I'm appreciative of my wife, Sandra, who served as my right-hand researcher and interviewer, and of my mother, Conaere, who served as line editor and provided invaluable encouragement. I've been blessed with a couple of researchers, Madison Watt and Kendaline Watt.

This book could not have been completed without the help of a number of law enforcement members, who are dedicated to keeping all of us safe and providing a quality of life that is underappreciated most of the time. First, DEA task force member and current City of Boca Raton police executive James Burke, who has been there since the beginning; former DEA agent Jim Hoy; former FBI agent Scott Rivas, a high school classmate; and all those who have worn the badge and pledged to make this a great country.

I'd like to offer special thanks to former Palmetto High coach Barry Zimbler; former Palmetto wrestlers Jeff Cutler and Mike Pedersen; University of Georgia wrestling coach George Reid; the team of journalists at the *Miami Herald*; my Skyhorse Publishing editor Ken Samelson; and literary agent B. G. Dilworth.

Finally, my rescue Belgian Shepherd Troy has sat next to my desk at home for hundreds of hours, including when I returned from visits at the depressing Miami Federal Prison. When Troy wagged his tail, he provided additional inspiration for me to share lessons learned from an era that should not be forgotten.

CHAPTER I

An Unlikely Friendship

He was impossible to miss. Impeccably decked out in an immaculately tailored white suit and carrying a walking stick (just for show, of course), Luis DeCubas made a characteristically magnificent entrance into the stands at one of the three baseball diamonds in Suniland Park. Every eye in the park was on him, exactly the way he intended, exactly the way he liked it.

He probably wouldn't have such a big splash these days, but you have to understand that he was far more of an anomaly back in the summer of 1970.

These days, Pinecrest—where Suniland Park is located—is a placid and affluent suburban town just southwest of Miami. Entry-level houses there start at about a million, and most of the population these days is made up of wealthy families of Cuban descent.

But back in 1970, it was more of a white-bread southern town, with far more in common with similar communities in Georgia or Alabama than the Miami region we know today. It was, as one resident recalled to me, little more than a two-lane highway and some houses. It was the kind of place where "you could still get hot dogs at the Burger King" if you wanted to eat out.

Not many men in Pinecrest back then would wear a suit to a kids' ball game, especially not one so fancy and eye-catching as the one Luis had on.

He was a big, not tall, just big man who was naturally and enormously strong. Silver-haired, exuberant, and extremely gregarious, Luis wanted to be everyone's friend. He loved his community, and he loved the United States of America. And he had good reason to.

Back in the '50s, Luis had been a pretty big deal in Cuba. And, at the time, Havana was the place to be. With gambling, nightclubs, and entertainment provided by the biggest names in show business, Havana was more Las Vegas than Las Vegas could even hope to be. It was wild, sometimes a bit lawless, but always a good time.

And Luis had been a big-time player there. He parlayed his preternatural sense of style, easy charisma, and ability to talk with just about anyone into one of the best gigs on the island as the fashion columnist for *El Habanero*, the city's most influential daily newspaper. He was welcome everywhere, barely ever paid for a drink, and was treated to the finest the fashion industry had to offer, free of charge. If a designer could get Luis DeCubas to wear his design back then, he knew it would sell.

It made him a good living, and Luis and his young family had an enviable house near the beach in Playa de Santa Fe, just east of downtown Havana.

Suddenly, it ended. After years of guerilla fighting, Communist rebels led by Fidel Castro stormed into Havana just after New Year's Day in 1959. By the end of the week, Cuban president Fulgencio Batista and some of his inner circle fled. The revolution had succeeded. Cuba was a Communist state and Castro was its unquestioned leader.

Things did not look good for high rollers like Luis. Communists don't exactly look kindly upon guys who bragged that they had a thousand different pairs of shoes. And when politicians, military officers, and even policemen with ties to the autocratic Batista regime started being executed en masse, Luis knew he had to leave or face the communists' wrath. He would later learn that his brother, Pedro, would be sent to a prison for little more than not being a communist.

Before Castro became embittered and hardline, he offered what he said was a pretty good deal for anyone who wanted to leave Cuba—they could go, but they could not take any belongings other than the clothes on their backs and the equivalent of five dollars in cash per family.

So that's exactly what Luis did. In 1960, he packed his wife and his two toddler sons onto an old British turboprop—one of the last commercial flights from Cuba to the United States for a generation. Luis made sure the boys wore matching suits for the occasion. The family landed in Miami, and Luis was determined to take his five lousy bucks and make a better life for his family than he could in Castro's Cuba.

He did it, too; but it wasn't easy. A media job was out. Although Cubans were steadily flowing into Miami, none of them had any money, and the media at the time didn't feel a need to try to sell them anything. And, back then, immigrants were expected to assimilate into mainstream American culture as quickly as possible. Spanish-language media didn't really fit into that scenario.

But he did know fashion. Through friends, Luis quickly got the first of several jobs in the retail garment trade. He worked night and day and, as his English improved, he moved up in the industry. Luis felt he had made it when he got a job at Austin Burke, one of Miami Beach's fanciest and most expensive menswear shops, in the summer of 1964.

The extra income allowed Luis's wife, Nena, to find them a gorgeous little house with an outdoor goldfish pond within walking distance from the store.

The boys—Alex, six, and Luis Junior, eight—were enrolled in North Beach Elementary School, in grades one and three. That was a bit of a problem, though. As hard as it might be to believe now, Alex and Luis Junior were the only Latino kids in the whole school. And, because they spoke Spanish at home, their English wasn't very good. Back then, that meant the boys were in a lot of fistfights.

Luis Senior had their backs. An old friend of Alex's recalls how he came home from school one day and asked his father what a "spic" was. At that, the old man burst into a fury, and told Alex that if anyone ever called him that to "punch him in the nose first" and then he would be there to defend him.

But Luis Senior knew he couldn't be there all the time, so he enrolled the boys in boxing classes at the Flamingo Park recreation center. The sport came to them easily. They were both natural athletes, had already had some experience defending themselves with their fists, and were both very big and strong for their ages. At the end of their first year in competitive boxing, both of the DeCubas boys had won their age class championships, in part because they were twice the size of the other kids they were fighting.

Neither ever forgot what Luis Senior told them over and over again: "Never let anyone beat you up, always have the last swing."

Nobody picked on the DeCubas boys anymore, especially Alex, who clearly had an inborn ferocity his brother lacked.

Luis Senior stood out in the stands at the field in Pinecrest. It wasn't just how he dressed, it was how he behaved. He had a smile and a kind word for everyone, was generous almost to a fault, and he was boisterous and loud, never holding back his contagious enthusiasm.

Many people in Miami Beach—and everybody who was any-body knew him—attributed his character to his Cuban roots. That's understandable, because in 1970, the area still wasn't very diverse. In fact, Luis was the only Latino many of the people there had ever met.

Other than the taunts the boys received in the early grades, his ethnicity never led to any problems or friction, though—at least none that anyone remembers. Everyone who remembers him now talks about how widely, even unanimously, beloved he was. His Cubaness was almost like a novelty to many in the area. It was kind of like having a real-life Ricky Ricardo from *I Love Lucy* in the neighborhood.

While his identity was as the local Cuban, Luis was eager to get his boys to assimilate. He knew that they could be part of their community through sports. Not only were they both talented enough to be successful, Luis knew that when they stood out, they would gain acceptance and friendships.

When he made his way into the stands at Suniland Park for the ballgame, it was all waves, handshakes, and pats on the back from the people who knew him, and stares from those who didn't. Nobody ignored Luis. They couldn't. He wouldn't let them, and they wouldn't want to.

There were plenty of people in the stands that day because Suniland was hosting the annual Little League all-star game. Two teams representing the best players in the area were facing off against each other.

Once the game started, eyes shifted from Luis to another DeCubas, his son Alex, who was on the mound. Like his dad, Alex stood out in Suniland Park, and not because of his Latino herit-age, either. Alex had grown into a very big boy, not that tall, just thick with muscle. He weighed in at approximately 160 pounds, or about twice as much as most of the other kids on the field. He had

originally wanted to play football, but the league in his neighborhood had a 145-pound maximum weight limit so that guys like
Alex wouldn't destroy the other kids.

He would have, too. Alex was a gifted natural athlete with the
ability to dominate and play through his own pain while dishing it
out to others without a thought. He didn't need to practice or lift
weights or even get in shape to be the best. He just showed up and
played better than anyone else at everything, including baseball.

Although he was facing all-stars, the best the community had
to offer, it sure didn't look like it. It would be cliché to say that he
looked like a man among boys out there, but it would also be true.

He wasn't throwing just a no-hitter or even a perfect game, he
was pitching what's called an immaculate game—he had managed
to strike out every single batter he faced. There was nothing fancy
about it, he just reared back, cocked, and fired. He threw nothing
but fastballs straight down the middle and dared the little boys to
hit them. None of them could.

After every one of Alex's pitches made an authoritative thud in
the catcher's mitt, every eye in the stands shifted back to Luis. He
was famous for his celebrations whenever Alex performed. After
every single pitch, Luis would stand and shout encouragement to
Alex. And, after every batter walked back to the dugout with his
head down, Luis would dance and yell more encouragement for his
son—all of it in Spanish, including his given name, Alejandro. He'd
shout "¡El Tigre!" from the stands. That's what he called his boy,
when it came to sports, the Tiger.

The people in the stands who knew him weren't offended, even if
it was their son who had just failed to even brush one of Alex's fire-
balls. Everybody knew Luis was that way; it was part of his charm.
And they had to face up to the fact that their boys were no match
for his kid. He was throwing smoke out there. They also knew
that, after the game was done, Luis would rush onto the field and

smother Alex in hugs and kisses. It wasn't strange or embarrassing, it was just different. Luis was Luis, and they liked him that way.

With two out in the bottom of the third, the next piece of fresh meat made his way to the plate for the home team.

Kevin Pedersen stood out almost as much as Alex did. While the rest of the kids on the field were about half Alex's weight, Kevin was more like a third. He wasn't just small, he was tiny; all gangly arms and legs even though he was the shortest kid out there.

He looked out of place at an all-star game, but he had earned the right to be there, playing as well as anyone in Pinecrest. He hit well, had the rare patience to draw walks, bunted, stole bases, and flashed some pretty slick leather at second base for the Suniland Optimists all season. Still, the manager had him hitting ninth.

Kevin made it to the all-star team because of one thing—hard work. Although he came from a family with more than a few athletic accomplishments back in Iowa, sports didn't come as naturally to Kevin as they did to Alex.

He compensated for a lack of size and innate talent with herculean effort. From the time he got up in the morning until the time he got into bed at night, Kevin was striving to get better, to be a champion. If he wasn't asleep, at the dinner table, or in a classroom, Kevin was running, lifting weights, or practicing his swing and double-play move. Nobody outworked Kevin.

His drive to win and be a champion, he realized much later, came from years and years trying to please his taciturn father.

Myron Pedersen had been captain of his high school wrestling team back in Des Moines, Iowa, and enlisted in the U.S. Army Air Corps days after graduation. When the United States became involved in the Second World War, he quickly became a fighter pilot, flying a deadly P-38 Lightning over the Southwest Pacific. It was his squadron—the 339th Fighter Group—that had the honor of shooting down a converted bomber that was carrying Admiral

Isoroku Yamamoto, the man who planned the attack on Pearl Harbor. Pedersen was not in the air that day, but historians credit him with downing one Japanese plane by himself on February 4, 1944, and for another kill shared with a squadron-mate later that year.

While it might sound successful, even glorious, on the outside, combat left Myron a changed man. He was just a wide-eyed twenty-one-year-old kid from the Midwest when he went off to combat. Deeply affected by the war—he saw two-thirds of the guys he shipped out with die—he suffered from what we would now easily recognize as post-traumatic stress disorder. But that wasn't a diagnosis back then. Something was wrong with him, everybody knew it, but there was no way to fix it. Instead, Myron withdrew into himself and started drinking. He'd pass out in his living room every night with his bottle of Seagram's 7.

Myron's condition made things tough for Kevin and his brother and sister. Their dad was never fun or close or affectionate. Kevin never once heard his dad say he loved him or that he was proud of him. "I grew up desiring, wanting his affection," Kevin said. "He did not know how to show feeling."

While Luis DeCubas was covering his son with hugs and kisses after even the slightest athletic feat, Myron would pick apart and criticize his son's performances, making a point of telling him why he wasn't a champion. "Sports was everything, my father instilled that in us at a very young age," he later said. "If you were going to live in my dad's home, you were going to be involved in sports." And expected to be a winner, a champion.

Kevin was deeply affected by the distant relationship he had with his father. The military life, with its rigid discipline and constant moving, also made it hard for Kevin to develop ordinary social skills.

After the war, Kevin's father attended Drake University on the G.I. Bill. He reentered the United States Air Force, making his way up to Colonel and he was assigned to several distant bases, often quite far away and culturally different from where he had previously been. Kevin was born in Châteauroux, France, moved to Spain, then to Massachusetts (where Myron taught ROTC students at Boston University), then to Ohio, then to California, and finally to South Florida when he was in second grade. Despite having two American parents, he was not a United States citizen until his father filed for naturalization because he was born off-base in a French hospital. "I can't be president," he later joked.

That lack of permanence in his early life made it hard for Kevin to make friends or even relate to the other kids. It wasn't that he was the weird kid, or at all unlikeable. He was just shy and kept mostly to himself. In fact, he had a problem with introversion that lasted well into his adult years.

All of those factors combined to push Kevin harder. Maybe too hard. His desire to become a champion had become an all-consuming obsession. "He demanded a lot, and I thought I performed a lot," Kevin said years later of his father. "Throughout my life I've been an overperformer; still trying to please someone who's been dead for fifteen years."

Baseball was a good fit for Kevin. Unlike some sports, such as soccer, that allow some kids to slack off while others steal the show, in baseball there's no place to hide. When the ball comes to you or it's your turn at bat, you have to perform and open yourself up to success or failure. That suited Kevin. Often overlooked, what he really wanted was a chance to show people what he could do, to show his dad that he was a champion.

His dad desperately wanted Kevin to play football. There was a league for kids his age that was limited to players ninety-five pounds or less. Kevin checked in at sixty-eight pounds. Even though he was nowhere near big enough to compete with the other guys, it was kind of an open secret in the park that if you sweetened the ten-dollar registration to the tune of, like, a hundred, your kid would make the team, no questions asked.

Kevin's father did, and on Saturday afternoons, he'd watch from the stands as his younger son had the stuffing beaten out of him from starting kickoff to game-ending whistle.

Finally, Kevin had had enough. Mid-game, he got up and walked home. His father chased him down and caught him. Incredibly angry, Myron asked Kevin how he could quit like that. Kevin explained that facing nothing but much bigger boys prevented him from succeeding or having fun. He couldn't understand why he had to get clobbered every week when his older brother, Mike, got to wrestle against kids his own size.

Myron was still angry at his kid for quitting, but he understood. He was withdrawn from football and enrolled in the same wrestling program—"in a warehouse out by the Bowl-O-Mat"—that Mike was already in.

When the batters came back into the dugout after Alex had put them down, they spoke openly and giggled nervously about how frightening it had been to face him. But not Kevin. He didn't make a sound.

Kevin made his way to the plate. He noticed, but didn't care about, the muffled muttering and discreet chuckling that the people in the stands felt compelled to do when they saw this tiny tyke on his way to challenge the young man who was dominating on the mound. That was fine, Kevin thought to himself. *Go ahead, underestimate me*, he thought, *I'll show you all what I can do*.

Luis was shouting: "¡El Tigre! ¡El Tigre! ¡El Tigre!" Myron just glared.

As Kevin assumed his stance, he locked eyes with Alex.

The big kid smiled and winked.

If this was a Hollywood movie, Kevin would have knocked the ball out of the park. But it wasn't. It was real life in suburban Miami. And real life is never predictable.

Instead of winding up, Alex called out to his catcher. The kid stood up. Alex used his left arm to signal him to move a step or two over to the left.

The crowd, even Luis, was dead silent as Alex did the unthinkable. He tossed a softie into the catcher's mitt, just out of Kevin's reach. There was a little nervous laughter. Kevin just grit his teeth and prepared for the next pitch. Alex did it again. And again, and again.

Kevin politely dropped his bat and trotted to first base, intent on stealing second and trying to figure out a way to score.

The crowd was confused. Nobody could understand why Alex threw away his perfect game to intentionally walk this little kid. They had never met before—Kevin went to Howard Drive Elementary School, while Alex attended Coral Reef a few blocks to the south— never even heard each other's names, so there's no way that Alex had any reason to fear or even respect Kevin's ability with the bat. Maybe he was mocking him or maybe he just thought it would be funny.

Years later, Kevin would tell me that Alex was "taking care of him." He believed that Alex had "such a big heart," that he always wanted to "take care of the little guy."

Kevin didn't score. Alex got the next batter out, and all the others he would face too. When he was finished, Luis came screaming out of the stands to hug and kiss the big boy. Myron watched sullenly as Kevin helped pack up his team's equipment.

After the game, Kevin and Alex hung out together. Kevin didn't ask why Alex intentionally walked him, and Alex didn't explain. Guys don't talk like that. At least, they certainly didn't in 1970.

But they did talk. In fact, they became friends. Right away, they both knew that they shared something. They didn't articulate that to themselves at the time, they just knew it.

Eventually, Kevin and Alex would become best friends. Luis would raise enough money to buy his own store just up the Atlantic

Coast in Coral Gables. He named it after himself, Don Luis, giving himself the honorific of a man well-respected in his community. Nobody would argue.

And that community would later be Pinecrest. As the boys got older, Luis and Nena wanted to give them more room and a better choice of schools. They moved to Pinecrest, and Alex and Kevin would become classmates, teammates, and friends.

But circumstances beyond their control would conspire with the very different households they came from to put them on a collision course, representing the opposing sides on the War on Drugs, each armed and ready to carry out their sworn duty should anyone get in their way—even if it was their best friend.

CHAPTER 2

Iowa Strong
and Cuba Proud

There was the faint sound of a bang, almost like someone slammed a door in a distant room. Someone smelled smoke. Then everyone did.

On an otherwise ordinary day at the end of May 1973, the kids at Pinecrest's Palmetto Middle School were rapidly surrounded by an acrid stench, then started to see a white cloud enter their classrooms, getting bigger and bigger.

Announcements came over the public-address system telling the teachers and students to remain calm, make their way out of the school as they had been taught, and that the fire department was on its way.

Then the alarms went off.

If there's one thing drilled into the head of public school teachers over and over again, it's what to do when they hear the fire alarm. Fire monitors were sent to search the washrooms, and to find the clearest path out of the school. The other kids were rounded up and led out of the building as quickly as was possible while maintaining order.

But the smoke grew thicker and thicker. It just wouldn't stop coming. No matter how low the kids got, they couldn't escape the school without breathing lungfuls of the stuff.

Once outside, many of the kids were coughing and vomiting. Some couldn't stand up, and just kept hacking and hacking while on all fours.

A few of the teachers, while doing their best to take care of the kids until the first responders got there, noticed there was something strange about what was going on.

There was a massive amount of smoke—it was almost like it was being forced out of the building by an unseen force even though there was no wind that day—but not even a hint of flame, or even heat. And the smoke didn't look or smell right. For one thing, it was bright white. There was no hint of burning wood or anything like that. It smelled like chemicals. In fact, it reminded some of them of the smoke grenades the police and National Guard used at the anti-war and civil rights protests that had gripped the nation for years.

That's because it was. Quickly, the school grounds were swarmed by first responders—fire trucks, ambulances, police cars, even a police helicopter showed up. The firefighters stormed into the school ready to douse a fire, but it rapidly dawned on them what they were actually fighting. They located the still-fuming metal canister in one of the gym's changing rooms, contained it, and brought it out of the school.

By that time, the media had arrived, and were interviewing students and teachers while taking footage of the ambulances ferrying away the fifty students who needed serious treatment for smoke inhalation.

It didn't take long to figure out that it was a late-in-the-school-year prank gone wrong. Some kid or kids had gotten their hands on a smoke grenade—erroneously reported in the media as a "smoke bomb," which is a much less intense iteration of the same general idea—and thought it would be funny to let it off in the gym. Clearly, their thirteen-year-old brains could not have understood how much damage it would cause.

It didn't take very long to find the culprits. Kids that age rarely have access to such sophisticated weapons. The canister was of the same kind that was in service by the Miami-Dade Police Department. One of the officers whose boy attended the school checked his equipment and, as he had feared, a smoke grenade was missing. He interrogated his son, who admitted to the prank, and quickly gave up the identities of his three co-conspirator classmates.

They all fell under the same type—rowdy to be sure, but not troublemakers, good athletes who had the discipline to get pretty good marks at the same time. They were what we would call jocks or future frat boys now, but back in 1973, they were just boys.

That presented a problem for school administrators. Sending fifty kids to the hospital was no laughing matter, but all four of the boys were good kids with bright futures. Despite the seriousness of what they had done, it just didn't make sense to mess up their lives. It was determined in an administrator's meeting that they would each spend a couple of weeks in a reformatory school, then return to Palmetto Middle School for graduation.

* * *

A couple of days after the incident, Barry Zimbler and his wife were driving back to Pinecrest after visiting some former students at the University of Florida upstate in Gainesville. He did that sort of thing fairly frequently. As head of the guidance department, football and wrestling coach at Pinecrest's Palmetto High School, he grew attached to many of his former students, especially his athletes and in particular, his wrestlers.

He had only been coaching wrestling for a few years—a recent retirement meant that the school needed a coach and since he already knew some of the guys from football, he studied the sport and took over—but he had grown to love it. There was something about the one-on-one competition, the striving to beat the other man with everyone watching your success or failure in the purest, most ancient form of combat that bred camaraderie among the wrestlers and their coach that other sports just could not. As Kevin would later point out, everyone on a football team, even the left offensive tackle, could take a play or two off here and there, but you just can't in wrestling. The coach, the other wrestlers, even the spectators see and assess every single thing wrestlers do. There's no place to hide, so you have to do your best from start to finish.

He not only loved wrestling, he loved his wrestlers and became something of a father figure to them. His teams were closer-knit than many families are, and many of his wrestlers went on to be successful later in their lives. "Wrestling is the toughest sport in high school, and the guys that come out of that are going to be successful," Kevin later said. "They don't even know what the word 'quit' is."

A little more than halfway home from Gainesville, the Zimblers stopped for a bite to eat—nothing fancy, just regular Southern cooking. He picked the place because it was nearing 6 o'clock, and because he knew the restaurant would be playing the local news on TV. He liked to listen to what was going on when he was eating.

On that very night, though, it was bad news—for him in particular. One of the small, local-interest stories they had on was about how police and school officials had rounded up the kids who lit the "smoke bomb" in the Palmetto Middle School gym. Since there were no laws protecting the identities of minors accused of crimes in Florida in 1973, the anchorman read off the four boys' names. One of them—that of Alex DeCubas—struck a chord with Coach

Zimbler. "Oh no," he thought, "that kid's going to be wrestling for me next year."

Indeed, he was, and so was Kevin Pedersen. Both boys had played a variety of sports, and both had chosen wrestling as their favorite.

Back then, middle school in the region went to ninth grade, and high school went for three years, meaning that Alex and Kevin entered Palmetto High as sophomores in the same class.

Alex loved wrestling not only because he was good at it, better than anyone he ever faced, but also because it was fun to knock the other guys around. Their junior high coach, Dan Dorshimer, positively gushed when he spoke to Zimbler about Alex. He had never seen, let alone coached, such a natural wrestling talent before.

Alex might have been Zimbler's star recruit, but Kevin was also at the top, also having gone undefeated in middle school. He was eternally grateful that it was a sport divided into specific weight classes. While Alex walked around at about 210 pounds, and he had to get down to a wrestling weight of 190 for competitions, Kevin had bulked up from the sixty-eight pounds he was when he started eighth grade to ninety-eight. Kevin used to laugh at how Alex complained about cutting weight to be eligible for his class, while he struggled to gain an ounce.

Their size difference meant that they would never face each other on the mat competitively.

Dom Gorie, a teammate of theirs who later became a space shuttle commander, recalled his reactions during an ESPN interview: "Kevin, when I first met him, looked like a grade schooler, hadn't reached puberty, just a little guy . . . had this baby face, thin, he was very quiet, couldn't engage him very easily, but he had that quiet confidence that you knew there was something lurking in there."

That confidence, in part, came from Kevin's inhuman workout routine, which would seem cruel if it were imposed on him by anyone else. "I would get up in the morning and run, I would go to school, I would run home from school, I would run back to practice, I had practice and, before I went to bed at night, I would run again, eat something, weigh myself then I would run again, then I would go to bed," Kevin said. "I ran and ran and ran, I tried to get beat up in practice, I never stopped lifting weights." Never a day off, rarely a moment off for the little guy who knew he could.

He also brought that same kind of dedication and determination to his school work. Described by several teachers and classmates as a "perfect student," Kevin brought home outstanding marks in every class. He was considered an exemplary student, never getting into the least amount of disciplinary trouble.

But academics took a back seat to sports. Actually, sport. Kevin was so dedicated to wrestling that he stopped participating in other sports. Sure, he'd throw the ball around with the guys if they asked, but the idea of taking another organized sport seriously was ridiculous—it would have gotten in the way of wrestling or preparing for wrestling.

That unquenchable desire to get the best out of himself came from his father—or, at least, his relationship with his father. Gorie told ESPN that he remembered the Pedersen boys' (Kevin and his big brother Mike) "whole personas changed" when they talked about their father. "He was extremely demanding," Gorie said of Myron. "He expected a level of perfection . . . not accepting anything that was not the best—a tough guy to be around."

That put Kevin on something of a vicious cycle. All he wanted was positive attention from his father. The only way to get that, he figured from what his father said and did, was to be the best at wrestling. To become the best at wrestling, he knew he had to work harder than anyone else. Kevin tapped into his inner drive, and nobody ever outworked him.

His preferred workout method, once inside the gym, incredibly, was to take on Alex. He'd start off every single practice by wrestling his big friend. And, while Alex had intentionally walked Kevin every single time he had ever faced him in baseball, he never went easy on him on the mat. They would go hard, full strength, and using every trick they knew. Kevin would invariably get pinned but he never really intended to win. He took the fact that he could even compete with Alex, a hundred pounds heavier, as a victory. And he knew it was making him a better wrestler. Going up against a guy like Alex, and getting his face jammed into the mat every day, would be like running with a hundred-pound weight on his back. Once the weight was off, he'd feel invigorated, and after wrestling with Alex, his opponents in the 98-pound class would seem puny, almost harmless.

It worked. Kevin was the undefeated junior high champion in his weight class.

And so was Alex in his. Nobody came close to pinning him.

But Alex didn't run unless he absolutely had to, he didn't really work out, and he certainly didn't go out of his way to find any bigger guys to wrestle. Alex just went out there, tried his hardest, and let nature take its course.

The first day of high school is stressful for anyone, but it was a lot easier for Alex than most. It's nice knowing that you could probably beat up anyone in the school if you needed to. But he also knew that he wouldn't have to, because his winning personality disarmed even the toughest guys.

Kevin, though tiny, was actually in a similar position. And if anyone he couldn't beat up ever gave him trouble, he always had Alex. Kevin never sought protection from Alex, it just happened. Alex was that way.

And nobody wanted to fight Alex. It wasn't just his size, he had a reputation. It was mostly based on one fight back at Palmetto Middle School. It was an eighth-grade physical education class, and the boys were playing "gator ball," which Kevin described as a mix between football, soccer, and rugby. It usually got pretty rough, and the teachers let the minor stuff go without any intervention. The school's other big kid felt that Alex had been a little too handsy, and made it clear he intended to fight. Instinctively, the other boys stopped their game and crowded around the two big kids. The fight didn't last long. As the other kid approached Alex, he unleashed a massive haymaker, knocking his aggressor to the ground and opening up a huge gash in his forehead. After that, everybody remembered that time "Alex split the other guy's head open," and decided that it was much wiser to avoid any physical confrontations with him.

By high school, a stern look or a proper word was more than enough to silence any challenger who wanted to pick on Kevin. "Everybody pretty much knew that you just don't say anything or do anything to Pedersen because DeCubas was always there," Kevin said.

And it was nice to get such a warm welcome to the school by Coach Zimbler, who had personally scouted them both, but was clearly more excited by Alex. "I went to Palmetto Junior High a time or two and watched him wrestle there," he said. "I couldn't wait until he'd arrive at Palmetto Senior High. I was excited to get him, always excited to get kids from Palmetto Junior High because they had a pretty good wrestling program, and we'd get pretty good wrestlers from there."

Indeed, they did. Zimbler knew the boys well in part because their older brothers—Luis DeCubas Junior and Mike Pedersen— were already on his team. Neither was the kind of star he expected Alex to become. They were just good, solid wrestlers.

The whole team was, and had been since Zimbler had taken over. And it was a huge deal back then.

High school sports were incredibly important to the communities in South Florida back then. Aside from the Miami Dolphins— who were still the toast of the region after their undefeated season and Super Bowl win a few years earlier—there were no professional sports in the area. No baseball, except for spring training, no basketball, and, of course, no hockey. The colleges drew plenty of fans, but mostly alumni and their families. For most people in South Florida, sports meant high school contests.

Some sports were more popular than others, and even those varied from community to community. In Pinecrest, wrestling had become by far the most popular, in no small part because of Barry Zimbler's success. It drew legions of loyal fans and plenty of coverage from the local media.

That loyalty, however, was tested by one fact that constantly ate away at Zimbler. As good as the program was, it had never won a state championship. They'd come close, and they had a number of individual state champions, but had never been able to bring home the hardware. Zimbler would later say he felt like he imagined the Dolphins' legendary quarterback Dan Marino must have; with all kinds of success and accolades, but no Super Bowl trophy.

The fans were polite about it, of course, but he heard the mutterings. The media—especially columnist Vin Mannix—were almost like boosters, but they could not have any credibility if they didn't mention the fact that Pinecrest had never won a championship. Zimbler felt like there would always be an asterisk beside his name in the record books, indicating that he could never win the big one.

Alex, he thought, could change that. He'd never seen such a natural talent. The kid was still very young, but strong as an ox, agile as a cat, and graceful as a butterfly. And he had more, something extra. He had the will and desire to impose himself on other wrestlers, and he was smart and spontaneously creative. Alex clearly had the talent to be the best wrestler Zimbler had ever coached—if he kept clean.

Zimbler knew all about Alex's discipline problems in junior high. He'd done his homework on the boy and as the head of the guidance department as well as his potential new coach, he had access to all the records that Palmetto Junior High had compiled on him.

Zimbler considered it a personal challenge to keep Alex out of trouble. And he succeeded—at least as far as he knew. "I know he had some problems in junior high school," he said. "But in high school, I don't remember him having any problems or I would've heard about it."

Of course, Alex's friends tell a slightly different story. He had a habit of getting in fights, in no small part because he knew he would always win them. Most of the people his own age who knew Alex mentioned a brawl he was in at a basketball game in nearby Opa-locka. As it is remembered, an opponent sent a Palmetto player to the floor. Alex leapt off the sidelines, prompting the benches to clear. In the ensuing melee, as the legend goes, Alex punched and elbowed his way to the opposing bench. There was only one kid there who didn't storm the floor, and that was because he already had a broken leg. But the kid decided to get involved in the fight anyway. As Alex ran by him, he swung his crutch at the big wrestler. Alex ran through the blow, breaking the crutch with his chest. Once he realized what happened, the story goes, Alex grabbed what was left of the crutch from the kid and started beating him with it before turning it on the rest of the Opa-locka kids.

But none of that made it back to Zimbler, apparently. "I can truly say that when Alex got to high school, he didn't have any problems from a disciplinary standpoint, because he knew I would've been all over him if he did anything that he shouldn't have done," he said. "He was very respectful. He was respectful of all the coaches, anything that we told him, he would do. He was a yes sir, no sir type of young man."

They were all "yes-sir, no-sir" kids at Palmetto. It was the '70s, and the use of illegal drugs among teens was rampant. Kevin later recalled walking through clouds of marijuana smoke on his way into Palmetto High. He claimed they were powerful enough to kill the clouds of mosquitoes that pestered the rest of the region.

Zimbler warned his wrestlers about the dangers of illegal drugs, especially Alex—not just because he was clearly the most prized of them, but he seemed to be more susceptible to something that might seem innocent and a little mischievous at first. "I expressed to Alex how I felt about drugs and how they ruined families and individual kids," he said. "And I gently shared my disdain about anyone involved with the drug scene." That made it personal: Start taking drugs, and you'd lose my respect, my affection.

Zimbler didn't have to worry about Kevin, though. Not only was he too busy for drugs or any other kind of illicit behavior with his workout routine, he had no interest. He was the straightest of straight arrows.

And he came by his wrestling prowess honestly. Kevin's mom, dad, and all four grandparents were from Des Moines, Iowa. And in Iowa, wrestling is king. It's what the state takes pride in and deservedly so. Iowa dominates the nation when it comes to wrestling. Since 1975, the University of Iowa has won the NCAA Division I team wrestling championship no less than 23 times—including nine straight from 1978 to 1986 and another six in a row from 1995 to 2000. The Hawkeyes have earned more than half of the national championships awarded since Kevin and Alex were in high school. Of the seventeen championships Iowa did not win in that period, rival Iowa State took two of them. To be a wrestler in the state of Iowa is to be something; many of them—even high schoolers—are local celebrities.

Before the war called them away, Myron Pedersen, Kevin's dad, was captain of the wrestling team at North High School in Des Moines and his brother-in-law was a Big 10 champion. "It's what you do in Iowa," said Kevin. "In my family, you had to know how to wrestle just to defend yourself."

It was, Kevin said, just a coincidence that the Pedersen family ended up in Pinecrest, which just happened to have one of the best wrestling programs in the state of Florida.

Even though Zimbler's teams were still without a state championship, they were easily the most popular athletic attraction on campus. "The first year I coached, we were 4–4, the next year, we were 9–3," said Zimbler, "and then after that it was unbeaten seasons, big-time scores, and people wanted to see that." In fact, more people came to Palmetto's wrestling matches than their football or basketball games. Matches would regularly draw more than a thousand people, about one in every ten Pinecrest men, women, and children at the time. Palmetto drew so many fans to its wrestling matches that they sometimes had to be relocated to the gym at South Dade Technical College just to contain them all. "The kids wanted to get in," Zimbler remembered. "They'd climb onto roofs and look through the windows." Even the cheerleaders would show up and perform without being asked.

Although Zimbler was overjoyed at the prospect of having Alex wrestle for him, he knew he was getting something special in Kevin as well. "Kevin was a 98-pounder their sophomore year," he said. "I love the Pedersen boys, always did."

And Kevin couldn't wait to get on the mat. He knew about Palmetto High's standard of excellence, and was excited to get a chance to contribute. He loved competition and thrived on it. He knew that Palmetto had strong wrestlers in every weight class, even his own, which was rare. He was also aware that they went "four-deep" in every class, but he knew, he said, that he was the best in his own.

Along with his dedication and workout routine, Kevin had an ace in the hole. Every summer, his family—"like a ritual," he said—would go back to Iowa. And when he was there, he was expected to wrestle. Not just the family. He attended ("not always by choice") wrestling camps for Iowans who expected to go to Division I wrestling programs and maybe even the Olympics.

The competition was beyond fierce. His brother Mike recalled that Kevin "came back a better, tougher Iowa-style wrestler."

It paid off. Kevin would frequently place fourth or fifth in his weight class in Iowa over the summer, but the skills he learned and the drive he acquired allowed him to have little problem going undefeated when he got back to South Florida.

As Kevin was becoming a better wrestler and trying to get closer to his father through their family roots and shared interests, the long trips to Iowa only furthered the social isolation he experienced. While the other guys were bonding, having fun, and chasing girls over the summer, Kevin was either in Iowa wrestling or in South Florida working out alone.

"I routinely would see Kevin running around the neighborhood. We'd be finishing practice, all tired, and Kevin would throw his stuff on and run home," said Palmetto High teammate Andrew DeWitt. "And it was year-round. I'd drive by the high school in the summer and there was Kevin out running laps."

Alex was not nearly as single-minded. He played every sport he could. He was an all-city nose tackle in football in the fall, and baseball in the spring. And he was capable in any sport, just using his natural athleticism and strength.

But his size, shape and ferocity made him singularly suited to wrestling. "My first memory of fourteen-year-old Alex was when I grabbed him, he was kind of like a bowling ball," said teammate Scott Sherouse, who was a couple of years older and also a heavyweight. "I would characterize him as a gorilla with the coordination of a ballerina." Even in Palmetto's much-vaunted program, Alex could beat anyone.

Everyone in the school was aware of Alex; he regularly got those little extras in life that those recognized as top athletes got. Teachers were generous with marks and would look the other way on the odd bit of mischief, while students who weren't simply in awe of him lined up to hang out with him.

That admiration wasn't limited to school. Luis Senior doted on his Tiger. He loved all three of his children, of course, but even a mild acquaintance could see that Alex was his favorite. They had an almost visible bond, and whenever Alex competed, Luis could barely contain his excitement and pride in his son.

It was reciprocal; Alex adored his father, and had nothing but respect for him.

It wasn't just his dad who was enamored with him, though. Everybody liked Alex. "He was one of those people, the kind that lights up a room when he enters it," remembered Mike Pedersen.

Alex had a ready laugh and was not shy about hugging anyone. "He was a good kid," said Zimbler. "Other athletes were drawn to him because he was a role model."

He might not have felt that way if he saw Alex's behavior away from wrestling practice. Alex's charm made him extremely popular, and he was not the type to avoid the temptations that provided. Alex liked to party and do all those things young men like to do when they are not thinking about their future. It would not be rare for Alex to leave the campus, see Kevin running his laps, go out and party and see Kevin again, still running, on his way home after a few drinks.

As different as they were away from the mat, Alex and Kevin had similar results on it.

Alex didn't let his social life get in the way of his wrestling. "He didn't back down, he was an aggressor," said Zimbler of Alex. "When the referee said 'Ready, wrestle,' *boom!* Here he'd come." He explained that it wasn't just his strength that made Alex so effective. It was his will to win, to never quit, to absolutely dominate his opponents.

The determination he showed on the mat was not just to show off and please his father. Friends said that Alex felt he could really do something special in wrestling, maybe even the Olympics.

And he could thank Zimbler for that potential. His practices were incredibly tough. Sometimes the kids would go thirty, even forty straight minutes of non-stop wrestling. They were better conditioned than any other wrestlers in the state, and they knew it. It was hard—Zimbler was fond of saying "I couldn't wrestle for myself," pointing out that the brutal conditions he mandated made a lot of guys quit the team.

But it was more than just the team's conditioning. Everyone who was asked about Zimbler years later said the same thing—he was like a father to the boys. He molded them into wrestlers.

As successful as they were, though, a state championship continued to elude Zimbler. "We were crushing teams in dual meets because of our solid twelve guys—we had a tough guy at every weight class," said Mike Pedersen. "The title of state champs just eluded us—it was always right there, but we'd be third, fourth, second again—to be that close and to know that, as a team, you could beat every single team in the state in a dual meet (and we did) . . . fate just kept pulling it away from us."

Things were starting to look up, though. Although the school was abuzz with the obvious potential Alex brought to the program, Zimbler and the other boys on the team were also aware of Kevin. Alex went undefeated in junior high, and so did Kevin. Alex was state champion in his weight class the year before, and so was Kevin.

The pair would have to wait, though, because Zimbler had laid down one sacred rule—no first-years on the varsity team. No matter how good they might be, they had to sit and let an upperclassman wrestle in their place. The reasoning was not just that the older guys had earned their way onto the team through years of hard work, but that their experience would be advantageous against

similarly seasoned opponents—rookie mistakes could not be toler-
ated on the Palmetto High varsity team.

Although he was ever the straight arrow and prepared to follow
orders to the letter, that rule did not sit well with Kevin. "I never
got a shot to play varsity," he said. "There's already a system built
up, and you're going to wrestle JV because you're in tenth grade."

From his first day of practice at Palmetto High, Kevin flashed
the kind of ability that made him stand out in junior high. "I know
I could have started, and I know I could have placed in the state,"
he said, then added. "I could have won the state." The other JV
wrestlers in his weight class were no challenge. Kevin wanted to
practice against the varsity guys in his weight class—to prove that
he was their equal or better—but Coach Zimbler forbade it. JV was
JV and varsity was varsity.

Kevin was quietly furious when he saw that Alex was given a
special exemption from that otherwise iron-clad rule. He, and he
alone among the JVs, was allowed to practice against anyone he
wanted. It would be a massive understatement to say that right out
of the gate as a fresh sophomore, Alex impressed—he left wrestlers
and coaches in awe. "This short, squat powerful kid was able to
do things physically that were beyond the comprehension of most
guys in the room," said Gorie. "He could take guys that were far
bigger than him, and he could throw them around like they were
grade school kids."

And not just with the junior varsity. In mixed practices, Alex,
at fifteen, was regularly dominating Zimbler's best seventeen- and
eighteen-year olds. It didn't matter what the situation was; from
top or bottom, Alex impressed not just with strength and aggressiveness, but with spontaneity and critical decision-making.

Palmetto High got off to a good, but not outstanding, start to
the 1974 wrestling season. They were winning, but they weren't
dominating. They looked less and less like champions even than the

previous teams that had come close but failed to grasp the ring. The criticism was getting louder and louder. Parents were talking, so were other teachers. The local suburban media took every opportunity it could to remind the people of the area, including Zimbler, that he had not won a state title, and it sure didn't look like he was going to this year. Even the mighty *Miami Herald*, the paper of record for South Florida, chimed in, pointing out that after its history of early success and lack of titles, Palmetto's lackluster start in 1974 did not bode well for breaking Zimbler's losing streak any time soon.

Zimbler reviewed his JV team. He looked at Alex. Nobody, no member of the varsity team, even those who were about 240 pounds, could last a minute with Alex. It was time, he realized, to break the rule. After the eighth match of the 1974 season, Alex was promoted to the varsity team.

During the regular season, Alex was undefeated. And the team was transformed. Alex wasn't just winning, he was destroying everyone. He was throwing guys around at will. Not one of his matches lasted long enough to be in doubt.

The fans went wild, none of them more than Luis DeCubas Sr. Although Pinecrest wrestling had enjoyed a dedicated fan base before Alex joined the team, afterward they were absolutely fanatical. Luis stirred the crowds up in a way the cheerleaders could only dream about. He would dance and shout, lead chants and most of all, bellow constant encouragement to El Tigre.

The feverish atmosphere at Palmetto matches reached a crescendo when they traveled to Stranahan High School in Fort Lauderdale for the state championship. Enough Pinecrest fans made the hour drive north so that they silenced the home crowd, many of whom had never seen anything like Luis and the show he put on ever before.

Although Palmetto was heavily favored, the ghosts of past championship losses weighed heavily on the crowd, the wrestlers and, of course, on Zimbler.

In those days, wrestling matches started with the lightest weight class and moved up through to the heavyweights because that's who everyone wanted to see. The Palmetto kid in Kevin's weight class— the one who had taken the spot that he thought that he deserved, had earned—didn't even make it to the tournament.

Things went really sour for Palmetto after team captain Mike Pedersen failed to make it to the finals. The partisan crowd fell silent. It was, they all knew, happening again. Zimbler's Panthers were falling apart exactly when they shouldn't. Another year, another almost championship.

Despite the gloom that hung in the air, Palmetto began to rally, taking a few more matches and qualifying for the finals.

It went back and forth, with no clear advantage by either team. The first Palmetto High wrestler to win his match in the finals was Jeff Cutler who defeated Jim Hume of The Bolles School (a renowned private school in Jacksonville) in a dramatic 5–4 overtime match.

As if the tension wasn't enough, the championship came down to the final match, the heavyweights. Palmetto was behind, but still had an infinitesimally slim chance to take home the hardware.

It's these types of situations of incredible stress and responsibility that separate the athletes from the true wrestlers. Alex was ready. "It's like something out of a movie," said Sherouse. "And it's an undefeated senior he's going against."

The task before this fifteen-year-old sophomore, still new to the varsity team, was immensely difficult. Not only did he have to beat the eighteen-year-old Joe Brown from Jacksonville's Jean Ribault High, who had absolutely dominated everyone up to that point, he had to pin him. Sherouse would later say that nobody expected him to win, let alone pin the guy.

Zimbler gave him a few words of encouragement. Witnesses would later say that Alex was so focused it appeared as though he didn't hear what his coach was telling him.

It started out as most predicted with the Brown, the big senior, controlling the match, using his size and wits to keep Alex off-balance and defensive.

But Alex wouldn't dream of giving up. He came storming back and, when the second period ended, the score was tied.

The senior opened the third period with confidence, and quickly had Alex reeling. With just about 30 seconds left, Alex dug deep inside himself. He knew he had energy reserves Brown clearly didn't. He put his head into his opponent's chest and began to turn him. It all happened so fast after that. Alex dug his feet in and exploded his lower body into his opponent. His man was on his back, Alex held him down for the pin.

Mike Pedersen, nearly inconsolable after his own surprise loss, did not watch the match. But when he heard the slap of a wrestler's back on the match, he looked over at Zimbler to see if the impossible had come true. Zimbler jumped from the sideline to go hug Alex. Palmetto won. They were finally state champs. The final score was 36.5–34.5 over Miami Coral Park High—a paper-thin margin in wrestling.

The partisan element of the crowd erupted in a cacophony of noise, tears and jubilation. Ignoring everything else, Luis Senior ran out of the stands to hug and kiss El Tigre, shouting all the time. The rest of the fans came tearing in after him.

Kevin, in the stands and wearing street clothes instead of the singlet he felt he should have been in, clapped politely for his friend's achievement. He was sincerely happy for his friend and his team. But he couldn't fight the feeling that he too should be celebrating a victory on the mat—his own.

Instead, he had to ride home with Myron, and explain again why Alex was allowed to wrestle varsity while he was still just on JV.

CHAPTER 3

Those Championship Seasons

"You ready, Ped?"

Nobody but Alex ever called Kevin "Ped." In fact, Alex had nicknames for everybody on the wrestling team—some complimentary and some decidedly not—and Kevin was Ped. Always Ped.

"You know I am," Kevin said, and assumed his opening stance. Even as he entered his junior year, Pedersen still looked like a little kid, all arms and legs in his barely fitting Columbia blue Panthers singlet. He had developed a habit of flipping his head to keep his boyish haircut out his eyes that made him seem even younger.

Across from him, Alex had bulked up and was even more solid than he was the year before. His upper arms were thicker than Kevin's thighs. He kept his curly hair short on the back and sides, as is commonplace with wrestlers, with long sideburns the only nod to the permissive era. He could easily have passed for an adult.

Nobody was ever late to Palmetto High's varsity wrestling practice. That's because it always opened with the main event—Kevin

Pedersen taking on Alex DeCubas. Every single day, the diminutive Kevin would challenge the gargantuan Alex.

Kevin lunged in for a takedown attempt. Alex dodged and tried to take advantage, going to Kevin's flank. But the little guy was too quick and was immediately behind the big bear. Alex reacted in kind.

The two went on like that, with Kevin lasting longer than almost all of Alex's heavyweight opponents. But finally, inevitably, Alex would get on top of Kevin and pin him.

"You're sweating all over me," Kevin complained.

"Maybe you'll get me next time," Alex laughed.

Just like everyone else in the gym, Coach Zimbler watched the whole spectacle with great interest. He admired Kevin's willingness to go up against an opponent he had no chance of beating, and he respected his skills and moves. But he couldn't help himself from concentrating on the amazing skills Alex had. Even against such an agile and quick opponent as Kevin, Alex's moves were pure poetry. The fact that such a big guy could do things with his body like that—it blew the veteran coach away every single time.

* * *

Life could hardly have been better for Alex on the way into junior year. He was charming, popular, and the one guy in Palmetto High that nobody, but nobody, ever messed with. And, he had just won the state championship in the school's most popular sport. It wasn't exactly a single-handed victory, but it was as close as you could get in a sport like wrestling. At the state championship, Alex had saved the day for the team with a dramatic and necessary pin, and the school appreciated him for it.

Comparatively, Kevin was just another kid. Sure, he got some recognition for his impressive feats as a JV wrestler, but most people just knew him as Alex's unlikely little friend who never stopped running and rarely had anything to say.

And friends they definitely were. They weren't exactly inseparable—Alex liked to party while Kevin spent his evenings working out—but when they were together, it was almost like they were uncomfortable being too far away from one another. Alex always sat next to Kevin in practice. Whenever they rode the bus, everyone else knew not to try to take the seat next to Kevin or Alex. And it was always the same, Kevin said years later, with "Alex talking, and me, beside him, being quiet."

They ate together at lunch every day and then hung out together in the schoolyard. Years later, Kevin recalled that Alex started taking an interest in tetherball. The pair of them would challenge any other kids who wanted to play, but it was never any contest. Alex's strength and quickness were just too much for any other kids to match up with. Kevin recalls that he rarely even touched the ball himself, but just about every time he played, Alex would hit it so often and so hard that his fists would start bleeding. And, Alex being Alex, he found that hilarious.

* * *

Scarcely bigger than he was the year before, Kevin was no more outgoing, and he entered his junior year essentially a nobody.

But at least he was on the wrestling team. It made him popular by default.

But along with the glory, there was also a huge amount of pressure being on the Palmetto High wrestling team in 1975. Long dominant, they had finally gotten the monkey off their collective back. They were state champions, and nothing else would satisfy the community but another and another.

Kevin, promoted to varsity, certainly appeared to be up to the

task. In the regular season, he went undefeated. To nobody's surprise, so did Alex. In fact, Alex did not let a single opponent work
his way into a second period.

Kevin had joined Alex among the South Florida high school
wrestling elite. He felt that there were no limits to what he could
do in his weight class, or even beyond.

One of his best assets was the fact that he had no problem maintaining his weight. Other wrestlers struggled to lose weight, mostly
water, to stay in their weight class. Kevin's brother, Mike, was one
of them. In order to stay in the weight class just above Kevin's,
he would go to great lengths to drop the necessary pounds. Kevin
later said that he thought his brother would have been much more
successful if he just moved up a weight class, instead of agonizing
about staying in his own class.

It was at one of those bouts when Mike was totally dehydrated,
trying to shed a few pounds by wearing a plastic sweatsuit (and he
also appeared to be suffering from a mild case of the flu), that Alex
sidled up to Kevin and said, "This is your opportunity to smoke
your brother."

Kevin didn't hesitate. He challenged Mike—bigger, older, and
the team captain. It didn't last long. "I tore into my brother," Kevin
recalled years later.

After pinning Mike, he felt a bit badly about it. "I knew there
was something wrong with me if I didn't beat my brother," he said,
pointing out that Mike was sick, dehydrated, and tired after a grueling practice, while he felt fresh as a daisy.

But Alex was having none of it. When Kevin put Mike down,
Alex leapt to his feet, shouting and cheering for his little pal. He
looked as though he couldn't have been prouder of him if Kevin
had just won a gold medal at the Olympics.

Both Kevin and Alex sailed through the regular season as juniors,
making it look easy. But then, for reasons he never understood,

Kevin lost in the semifinal of the state championship. And so did Alex. And so did Palmetto High. The final score was a heartbreaking 36.0 for Stranahan High to 33.0. The only Palmetto High wrestler to win his class was Jeff Cutler.

It was a huge blow to the program and to the boys. Neither Kevin nor Alex had ever lost a competitive wrestling match up until that point, going back to the time when they were scarcely older than toddlers.

Predictably, it made both of them vow to come back even stronger. "Well, that loss turned out to be a real blessing for me," Kevin later said, "because it changed my whole thinking of I'm not going out to wrestle not to lose any more, because [then] I've already lost. I'm going to go out there and win. Every match I wrestle, I'm going to win. I'm going to beat the crap out of them. I'm not even going to think about losing. If I lose, I lose, so what? Now I'm going to win, and I'm going to win with gusto."

Although they probably didn't need any more incentive, Coach Zimbler felt that he knew exactly what to do to get his star wrestlers back on track, to provide an extra boost to their already competitive natures. Although they were two very different boys, he felt that they would be encouraged by the same thing. At the start of their 1976 season, he named Kevin and Alex co-captains. Kevin, he knew, craved both responsibility and duty, while Alex had his own needs, thriving on fame and acknowledgement. Both would get what they wanted once they were elevated a little bit above the other wrestlers.

But Zimbler miscalculated just a little bit. While the father-figure coach was raining praise and affection over Alex, he treated Kevin far more distantly. Perhaps he thought that Kevin's own introversion would have made any warmth from him feel awkward. Kevin, increasingly isolated, in fact desperately wanted the very tenderness that he never got from his own father. "What I got from Coach

Zimbler was appreciation and recognition," he said. "I needed that as a young man, but I think what I wanted more from him was affection." That was exactly what Alex got naturally, and in immense amounts. It was almost as though Zimbler behaved towards the boys in a rough caricature of the way their own fathers did.

Of course, there would be no slacking off the workout routine for Kevin. He continued his grueling exercise program and still started every practice with an all-out match against Alex. The outcome was inevitable, of course, but Kevin took great pride in lasting as long as he could and scoring points off his colossal opponent. "He would always beat up on me at the beginning of practice, it was Pedersen and DeCubas wrestling," he recalled years later. "Of course, he'd hammer me, just kill me; we were probably about a hundred pounds different."

His daily poundings at Alex's hands were part of a long-range plan on Kevin's part to be a better wrestler—and it paid off. Going up against Alex in practice as well as the very best Iowa could offer in the summer had transformed Kevin into something of a wrestling machine.

One of the fundamental rules he learned was that wrestling was not just about strength, timing, and technique. It was a mental and emotional war of dominance or submission. And he learned that the best way to win a match was to hurt your opponent so much that he just couldn't continue any more. It wasn't cheating, he decided, it was wrestling the way it was intended. "There are little tricks you can do to punish a guy," He said. One of his favorites was to bash an opponent's eye socket with his forehead, which he knew caused intense pain, but was generally not called as a foul. Because of his placid demeanor away from the mat, every time he'd pull a stunt like that, the other wrestlers were surprised—*Did Kevin really do that?*

Whatever frustrations he had in his personal life, he took out on his opponents. After lasting as long as he could against Alex and competing with all those competitive guys back in Iowa, the best of what South Florida could put up against him in his weight class didn't stand much of a chance at beating him. As a senior, in the regular season, he again went undefeated.

And so, of course, did Alex. In fact, Alex again didn't have a single opponent escape the first period all year.

To the surprise of nobody who was paying even the slightest amount of attention, when it came to the state championship for 1976, both Kevin and Alex made it.

Kevin had the good fortune, he would later say, to face the only person in his weight class ever to beat him in Florida—"a guy named John Minskey from Largo," who knocked him out in the semifinals in 1975, even though he had moved from the 98-pound class to the 105.

Years later, Kevin recalled that he "enjoyed every single second" of that match. He was in such good condition that he didn't even break a sweat to put Minskey down. Kevin, in his final high school match, had become state champion.

After celebrating with his teammates, Kevin looked up into the stands. As his senior season progressed, Myron had taken to walking out of the bleachers and onto the floor after Kevin's wins, and shaking his hand to congratulate him. But this time, without any words, he actually hugged his son in front of everyone. It was the first time that Kevin realized that his dad was genuinely proud of him, and was unable to prevent himself from showing it. He didn't say anything.

Myron had always drilled into his son that he wanted him to be a champion, and now he was. Throughout it all, Kevin's goal had been to be state champ, and he did it, while going undefeated. It was the culmination of all those countless hours of running and training, the intense weightlifting, the total disregard for a social life, all the trips to Iowa and their fierce matches and all those pins from Alex. Years earlier, Kevin had set out to win his dad's respect and affection, and had done it in spectacular fashion. His reward wasn't a trophy or his name in the local paper. It was that one very public hug. He later called the moment one of "vindication."

Kevin's success set the tone for the rest of the Panthers that evening. They were well poised for the state title when it came to be Alex's turn.

Just as he lost in 1975 after Kevin did, in 1976, he put on a terrific performance to match Kevin's. Alex dominated Miami Carol City High's James Gilbert from the start and pinned him before the first period was even close to ending.

Luis, who had been dancing and shouting to El Tigre throughout, shot out of stands and was hugging and kissing his son before his opponent had even gotten off the mat.

It was all over. Both Alex and Kevin finished the state final, and their high school careers, as champions. Palmetto High had taken the state championship again. It was Zimbler's second title in three years. And it wasn't even close. Even the lopsided 85.5–53.0 margin over runner-up Miami Killian doesn't properly indicate how dominant Palmetto High was that day.

He had been right about Alex, and he had been right about Kevin, even if he had been a little late in unleashing his prime weapons. When it was all said and done, the history books would forever read that Alex had earned an 88–1 record, while Kevin went 63–1. As remarkable as those numbers were, each boy's win total could easily have been in the nineties if only Zimbler had relaxed his rule about first-years not being allowed on the varsity team earlier than he did. Remember, both Kevin and Alex had gone undefeated in JV. And it should also be noted that Alex separated his shoulder in two matches, both of which he won.

The wrestlers were the toast of the school as they never had been before. They walked around the halls of Palmetto High like they were rock stars. Of course, the bulk of the admiration went to Alex, the face of the program. Not only was he the heavyweight—and that's always the star attraction in combat sports, when the big boys square off—but he had been the big man on campus at Palmetto High essentially from the first day he showed up. Besides, he was everybody's pal, a good guy who was always up for a laugh or a fun time.

Even Kevin got caught up in the groundswell of positive feelings after the championship. He got a few more hellos and the odd pat on the back, but it didn't matter to him. He'd already achieved his goal of being a champion and receiving his father's grudging approval.

Things were changing for Kevin in his senior year, especially after the state championship. He even started dating a girl from his class, Betty Atkins, pretty seriously.

The aura of accomplishment that had been surrounding the wrestlers was not even beginning to dissipate almost two weeks after the title when Zimbler saw Kevin in a hallway and called him into his guidance office. When he walked in, he could see that Alex was already waiting inside. Kevin shot his friend an inquisitive look, and Alex responded with an I-have-no-idea look, the facial equivalent of a shrug.

Zimbler sat behind his desk, facing the boys, and was absolutely beaming. "Just to let you know," he told them. "We sent something off and you're going to be in next month's *Sports Illustrated*."

People who were not alive in the middle 1970s would find it almost incomprehensible how big a deal that really was back then. Americans at the time had the same huge appetite for sports and sports news as they do now, but there was a dearth of actual sports media, and practically no national or international sports media. There was no Internet, no ESPN, nothing even remotely like that. As hard as it is to believe now, very few NFL games were televised nationally, let alone the less popular sports. Other than *Wide World of Sports*—a long-running Saturday afternoon sports anthology show on ABC—the only significant national media outlet was *Sports Illustrated*. There were a couple of other upstart sports magazines, but *SI*—which The *New York Times* said was responsible for "popularizing sports" in America—gave away more free copies for promotion than the others sold. To appear in *Sports Illustrated* was huge. It was the absolute pinnacle.

And it was theirs. A couple of pages into the March 29, 1976 issue—the cover featured Indiana center Kent Benson sinking a dunk on Marquette's Earl Tatum—was their names. In the front of every issue, was a feature called Faces in the Crowd, which presented outstanding achievements by amateur athletes. Their listing, the longest, read:

> Kevin Pedersen and Alex DeCubas, seniors at Miami Palmetto, ended their high school wrestling careers as Class AAAA state champions in their respective weight divisions, and led the Panthers to the Florida team title. Pedersen, at 109 pounds, had a career record of 63–1 in two years of varsity competition. DeCubas, at 189 pounds, compiled a three-year record of 78–1, including the 1974 state title. Undefeated in 33 meets this season, each contributed 17½ points to the record total of 85½ scored by the Panthers at the state meet.

A careless copy editor appears to have cheated Alex out of 10 career wins, but that didn't matter much. It was impossible to deny what the boys had accomplished.

Being mentioned in *Sports Illustrated* was, in itself, a newsworthy event pretty well anywhere in America back then, and the local paper sent a reporter to interview the boys and a photographer to snap their picture.

They were on top of the world. Wrestling had brought them everything they could have wanted out of their three years of high school.

Alex became the best-known and most liked kid in school. He was a celebrity, and he walked around Pinecrest with the same self-confident swagger that his old man did back in Havana.

Kevin was a champion, the only thing he wanted to be because he believed that would win him his father's respect and affection, symbolized by a single hug.

And the time and effort they put into wrestling would keep on giving. Their accomplishments on the mat meant that neither boy would have to pay for a top-notch college education. Full-ride scholarship offers from highly desirable universities kept arriving in the mail—some, no doubt, prompted by the mention in *Sports Illustrated*.

Alex selected one of the most academically prestigious schools in the region, the University of Georgia at Athens. The fact that it is also renowned as a first-rate party school probably did not elude him, either. He wasn't entirely certain about what was ahead of him, though. He'd go to Georgia, try to do well in his classes, take wrestling more seriously—everyone was telling him he had a legit shot at representing the United States at the Olympics in Moscow in 1980—and have himself a good time.

Kevin, as expected, took another route. The straight arrow politely examined and considered every scholarship offer, but he knew right from the start of the process exactly where he was going to go to school—the United States Military Academy, better known as West Point.

But it almost didn't happen. He had received plenty of offers from colleges, even Ivy League schools, but had decided to limit his choices to one of the major military academies. He had applied to West Point, but no answer came. He checked the mail every day, but nothing came. He was prepared to accept an offer from the United States Naval Academy—where his brother, Mike, was already enrolled and becoming a bit of a star on their boxing team—but held on, waiting for the envelope he so wanted.

When an offer finally came in from West Point just before he was about to give up hope, Kevin couldn't reply fast enough. Although he was effectively throwing away tens of thousands of dollars in offers from other schools—West Point does not charge students for tuition, room, and board—Kevin didn't care. Heck, he thought, they even pay me.

He saw his future in front of him clearly. He wanted nothing more than to become an officer in the United States Army. But he still held out hope for the Olympics as well. Aware he'd never make the US team because of the competition he'd face in his weight class from the guys he knew from Iowa, he realized that he was eligible to wrestle for France—he had been born there and was still a dual citizen—and thought he was probably good enough for their squad.

For the first time since they were little kids—although it could be argued if Alex was never truly little—they would be separated. Kevin would no longer have Alex to push and protect him. Alex would no longer have Kevin to set a positive example for him.

They would leave behind the idyllic life they had as high school champions to face the trials of college life away from home, from their fathers, and from each other.

Both Kevin and Alex would suffer through great tests of their character over the next few years, and both would emerge as men very different from the boys they were, but entirely composed by what they had been up until then.

Before all that happened, though, Kevin and Alex had the rest of the school year to bask in their accomplishments. They'd both won, they'd been in *Sports Illustrated*, they had free rides to essentially whichever college they wanted to attend, and both had, in their own way, made their dads proud.

CHAPTER 4

West Point Blues

Kevin was at the end of his rope. Never in his life had he been anywhere near as desperate as he had been at the start of his first year at the academy. West Point had, as it had to so many other bright-eyed young students over the decades, done a number on him.

It just wasn't working out for him. His marks were so low that he was on the verge of flunking out. The fact that he just couldn't cut it at the academy filled him with shame, humiliation, fear, and self-loathing. He'd never actually failed at anything before, and this was the very thing he had wanted to succeed at for a very long time.

Believing that he was without any other option, he decided that he would have to quit the school. He didn't have any idea what to do with his life after he left the academy, but he knew he wanted out of West Point more than anything else. He wanted to leave before they got rid of him, just to save a little face. Once he was back home in South Florida, where things made more sense, he told himself, he could figure the rest out.

It was with a shaking hand and eyes welling up that he made the phone call that would change his life. Kevin called his dad.

After telling him all the details of his situation, he told him point-blank: "I'm quitting West Point."

Myron was quiet for a moment, as though he was considering what his son had told him. He had been against Kevin's going to West Point in the first place. He was a career Air Force man—the air corps was part of the army when Myron joined, but it became its own branch in 1947 and the two branches have been rivals ever since. Mike attending the Naval Academy wouldn't make matters any better.

Kevin was sure that Myron would start with something like "I told you so," but what his father actually said stunned him, and made his blood run cold.

"You can quit if you want," Myron told him. "But you can't come here." Then he hung up.

* * *

Kevin thought he knew discipline after growing up in a military household. And he thought he knew what it was like to be isolated, alone, and without control because of the distance between him and his demanding father, his own introversion, and the fact that he had chosen hard work in both athletics and academics to a social life. But he had no clue what was in store for him a twenty-hour drive north from Pinecrest.

The polite term at West Point for a first-year student is *plebe*. It comes from the Latin word *plebian*—what the Romans used to call their lower-class citizens, people without power or any connections through family, friends, or personal currency.

That's the polite term. More frequently, however, first years like Kevin were known as "smack." It has far less classical origins. At West Point, it's an onomatopoeia meant to mimic the sound of a piece of shit falling from the back end of a horse. *That's what we think of you, first year, to us, you're a piece of shit.*

"Every cadet goes in there at the top of their class, the top of their game," Kevin said. "And they want to very quickly let you know you're smack . . . they break you down."

The purpose of the rough first year is to relieve the cadet of any feelings of superiority or undue influence he might have shown up with and to remind him that the army knew better than he did, and it was his time to learn, not share his own opinion.

West Point certainly had broken Kevin down, maybe too far down. The upperclassmen showed Kevin little, if any, mercy. Here was this quiet little Southern kid who looked too young to have gone to high school, let alone college—even though he had bulked up to 118 pounds by then.

It was a shock. Kevin had never known bullying—he could usually take care of himself physically. And, if he couldn't, there was always Alex. Everybody knew you couldn't say anything about Kevin, even look at him the wrong way, without suffering the wrath of mighty Alex.

At West Point, though, the bullying was constant and it came from every angle, as though it was an institutionalized part of the school's culture. Kevin knew he couldn't fight back, and there was no Alex there to help him out, either. Always a sensitive and conscientious boy, Kevin took every bit of criticism to heart.

But it wasn't them that presented the biggest challenge for Kevin. Sure, they laid into him pretty hard, but they were also busy harassing the girls—West Point began admitting female cadets the year before Kevin's class, and they were still a novelty to some. To others, they were a black mark on the school's history and culture and had to be driven off before they could do any further damage. As bad as Kevin had it, the first girls at the United States Military Academy had it far worse.

Actually, Kevin's big problem was his own expectations. He had wanted to go to West Point since he was a grade-schooler. He said he felt a need to serve his country, to serve others. As a child, he had entertained several ideas for his adult career, all of them in a public service capacity. He narrowed it down to police officer, firefighter, or soldier; although he had once considered long-haul truck driver "so I could be by myself," but crossed it off the list because he considered it selfish. When he learned about West Point with its history, traditions, and prestige, the other potential careers were dropped. Kevin decided then and there he was going to go to West Point to become an officer in the United States Army.

Kevin being Kevin, he was dedicated to that idea to an almost ridiculous degree. When all the other guys he knew had posters of Farrah Fawcett, Cheryl Tiegs, or other pretty models in their bedrooms, Kevin actually had one of the West Point campus.

He later said that the military appealed not just to his altruistic nature but also because he considered it "safe." While many might think that would be a poor word to describe military life, to young Kevin, the hierarchy, structure, and discipline of the army kept him safe from any uncertainty, which he feared far more than getting shot. He had grown up believing that the army would be where he fit best.

So, it was a brutal shock when he found out that he didn't fit at West Point at all.

Back at Palmetto High, he found that it had been easy to regiment his time. He'd wake up early, run, go to school, practice, lift weights, run, eat, run some more, and go to sleep. For him, homework was a breeze. He'd usually finish it all before the school day even ended. If not, he could always find the time. He was, as they say, a straight-A student.

And then he experienced the cold-water-to-the-face change in lifestyle cadets get when they enter West Point. Their decision-making was about as welcome as their opinions. Time was no longer their own. They were told when to wake, when to eat, when to study, when to practice, and when to sleep. And there is always something for cadets to do at West Point. There was drill, K.P. and all the other duties required to keep the school going as well as their studies and extracurriculars.

Deprived of the ability to make his own schedule, Kevin fell sorely behind in academics and in wrestling.

Palmetto might have been considered something of a destination high school in South Florida, but it wasn't at all academically rigorous by the standards West Point expected. Kevin experienced something of a culture shock when he first arrived. "Some of these kids from the Northeast were so far ahead of me academically, that I was at the bottom of the totem pole," he said. "We were all graded on a curve, against your fellow students, and I was finding myself at the bottom of the curve." At West Point, he noted, you can fail a test if you score 90 percent on it if everyone else scored higher.

After US involvement in the Vietnam War conflict ended in the middle 1970s, there had been a massive surge in applications and enrollment at West Point. The school became even more crowded after Congress ordered it re-admit more than a hundred students who had been kicked out over their involvement a cheating scandal. It was widely known that the school was over-strength, swollen with too many students, and everyone there knew that failing even a single course would give the powers that be enough reason to get rid of one.

West Point was hardly kind and nurturing to those who fell behind back even before the overcrowding crisis. The cadet with the lowest marks in every class faced expulsion. And the instructors made no secret of who was in trouble, either, posting every student's rank in their classrooms. The desk in the farthest left in the back row of every classroom was reserved for the laggard. Everybody knew it. They called it the "ejection seat," because if you sat there long enough, you'd be thrown out of the school.

Kevin found himself being forced to take the ejection seat in just about every class he took. His lowest marks were actually in computer programming, which was surprising because Kevin had actually worked long and hard to convince the school to allow him to use it to fulfill their foreign language requirement. His reasoning was that Fortran, the computer language the class taught, was just as foreign to him as any other language. They bought it.

When he saw his marks slipping toward the bottom, it didn't take long for him to realize that his days at West Point appeared to be numbered.

And then it came. Every West Point cadet feared hazing, expulsion and a variety of other problems, but nothing struck terror into them like the Dear John letter. Going to West Point is a lot more traumatic to high school relationships than going away to other colleges—even though that can be profound as well. West Point puts a bigger barrier than just mere physical distance between sweethearts. Because cadets' time is so highly regimented, contact with family and friends off campus is limited to a mere trickle. And there's no spring break or long weekends or anything like that, cadets are expected to be at West Point every day of the school year except for a short vacation around Christmas and New Year's. High school romances fall apart for first-year West Point cadets at a terrifying rate.

As busy as he was at Palmetto High, Kevin had a serious girlfriend in his senior year. He might have been shy and small, but he was also nice-looking, considerate, and a member of the prestigious wrestling team. He and Betty Atkins had been sweet on each other for a while, and in senior year they started dating.

As soon as the rest of his squad at West Point found out Kevin had a girlfriend, they started counting the days until his Dear John letter came, frequently reminding him it was only a matter of time until the sad news arrived.

West Point has a funny little tradition for when a cadet receives his Dear John letter and when Betty sent hers to Kevin, the other eleven guys in his squad—as was the academy's custom—signed her letter and left messages on it congratulating her on being rid of him and assuring her she made the right decision and mailed it back to her.

It was too much for Kevin to bear. All of the things that he held dear in his life were being taken away from him one by one. And everybody appeared to be laughing at him while it happened.

Calling his father to tell him he was quitting was the hardest thing he had ever done.

But after Myron rebuffed him in no uncertain terms, Kevin was dumbfounded. He had made no other plan other than to leave West Point and go home. It was too late to try to get another scholarship at another school. Maybe he could go to junior college and try to get back on track, but he had no money. Kevin knew that his dad was serious—if he left West Point, he would be homeless.

Terrified, he then made another phone call—this one to Coach Zimbler. Kevin told him everything. "Kevin, you're exactly where you need to be," Zimbler told him. "You've just got to suck it up."

He was right, and Kevin knew it. He had dedicated his life to this dream, and he had to make it work. Sure, he was behind the other cadets academically, but he had to believe that he could turn it around.

That meant he had to dedicate himself to his schoolwork and nothing else in order to keep from being expelled. The only bargaining chip he had left was wrestling. In order to make more time for academics, Kevin realized he had to give up wrestling.

Sure, it was a difficult decision, but when your heart has been broken into so many pieces already, a few more cracks isn't going to hurt that much. Besides, he had injured his shoulder again and was beginning to realize his dream of making the Olympics would never materialize. He knew he was not able to compete at the top of his weight class in the US, and West Point forbids its students from competing under any other flag, so wrestling for France was out.

Kevin manned up and apologized to LeRoy Alitz, West Point's legendary wrestling coach, then told that him that he had to withdraw from the team. Alitz was, as Kevin recalled, "mad as a hornet." But he understood, and reminded Kevin that academics were more important, and that since he had chosen West Point he didn't have a scholarship to lose if he left the team.

"I knew I needed to graduate from West Point," Kevin later said. "And I knew if I kept on wrestling, it wasn't going to happen." He later described the agonizing choice as feeling like he had part of his heart "ripped out."

Quitting varsity wrestling at West Point also meant that Kevin was banned from participating in intramural wrestling. That effectively meant he was never going to wrestle competitively again.

Ego solidly in check, Kevin approached his professors in search of help. To his utter surprise, they worked with him graciously and with great dedication. He gradually moved out of the ejector seat, and closer to the front of the class. At the end of his first semester, Kevin's lowest mark was a C. After that, he said, he really began to grow.

Kevin had made an agonizing decision. "Wrestling was gone," He would later say. "And it wasn't coming back."

But in that decision, Kevin found out who he really was. Wrestling had made him friends (even a girlfriend), it had made him tough and strong, it made him popular at school, it had gotten him college offers and, most important, the respect he craved from his dad. But it was time to put it away now. Kevin wasn't at West Point because he was a wrestler. He was there because of his marks, his interview, and his character. Cadets need a member of Congress to sponsor them in order to be accepted, Kevin's was then-President Gerald Ford.

Kevin knew he had to move on with his life. He was no longer a wrestler; he was a student and he was a soldier.

He took those roles seriously, and became something of a model student, just as he had been at Palmetto High.

By Kevin's senior year, he wasn't exactly at the top of his class, but he wasn't far off, either. He had gained the respect of his instructors and his squad. Kevin Pedersen was, as Coach Zimbler had assured him, exactly where he belonged.

And he had changed. The treatment he had received at West Point had worked exactly as it was intended. Kevin developed a thick skin and the kind of quiet confidence that comes from accomplishment and dedication to the duty to a higher cause than just yourself. And he was no longer the introvert who arrived there nearly four years earlier. "West Point took that right out of me," he said. "They forced it out of me, and I'm thankful for that."

It was just before Christmas in 1979 that Kevin received another letter from South Florida. He was surprised to see that it was from Betty, his old high school sweetheart who had broken his heart in his first year away.

In it, she told him that she missed him, and very much wanted to talk with him.

As soon as he could, Kevin ran to one of the campus pay phones and filled it full of coins.

After some pleasantries, she explained that South Florida had changed, and that it was all because of drugs. Kevin thought he knew a lot about drugs, but he didn't. The kids at Palmetto High, when he was there, smoked a lot of weed, a few of them took pills such as Quaaludes or Valium and one or two had experimented with LSD. Heroin, he knew, was a problem in some places, but not really in Miami, certainly not Pinecrest. Kevin, of course, didn't partake in any drugs, of course, but he considered himself aware of the situation.

Everything changed, she said, when cocaine came to town. Kevin was only obliquely aware of cocaine. It had been legal at the start of the twentieth century, and even added to over-the-counter pain pills and soda pop (it's how Coca-Cola got its name), but had fallen out of favor. Associated mainly with poor African Americans and psychotic, often illegal behavior, cocaine was outlawed in the United States in 1922.

It had faded from public consciousness by the time Kevin was born. But in the early 1970s, coca farmers in Peru started making deals with Colombian smugglers who had been moving weed and other products like gemstones and even coffee through the Caribbean to the United States.

To them, it was like finding a goldmine. To the Colombians, Cocaine was the perfect product to smuggle. Unlike marijuana, effective doses of cocaine were tiny, and easy to conceal—and back then, most airport and border crossing security was a joke compared to today. Cocaine made people happy, at least in the short term, by giving them energy, self-confidence, and an increased sex drive. And, best of all from the point of view of the traffickers, it was extremely addictive. People who tried it almost invariably wanted more and more and more. They would pay anything, do anything for another bump.

It caught on, first in New York, then in Miami, then the rest of the country. Cocaine use was associated with wealth and style by the disco generation, which guaranteed it was going to be both popular and expensive.

There seemed to be no limit to how much people would pay for a snort of the stuff. Cocaine trafficking could turn a nobody into a millionaire in no time. Once people saw their friends driving around in Ferraris and wearing Rolexes on their wrists while working a couple of days every few weeks selling coke, trafficking became a desirable career path with no shortage of eager applicants.

But that ridiculous amount of easy money brought with it intense competition. And those who established themselves, mostly the Colombians, were bad dudes who meant business. Miami, Betty told Kevin, was not what he knew it as anymore. People were shooting each other left, right and center. It was too dangerous to leave the suburbs, and it wasn't even truly safe even there.

The Dear John letter she had sent him when he was a plebe, she explained, happened because she had met another guy, Steve Zalinsky. She had always loved Kevin more, she maintained, but felt like she really couldn't put her life on hold for four years, waiting for him to come home to South Florida or wherever the army was going to send him.

She started dating Zalinsky, she said, even though he was about eight years older than her, and they eventually married and had a son, Daniel. Kevin congratulated her and wondered to himself what any of their conversation had to do with him.

Things were not good at home, she said. Like pretty much everyone in their generation in South Florida, both Betty and her husband started taking cocaine. It was great at first, she told him, but it took a huge toll on both of them. In order to pay for their own cocaine use, her husband started selling.

That only made it worse. With cocaine always around, Zalinsky started to use more and more. It made him different, angry, suspicious, paranoid, even violent.

That was it, she told him, she had to do the right thing for herself and her boy and leave him. She moved back in with her parents and went through the long and difficult process of getting clean.

She told Kevin that she no longer used drugs, no longer wanted them, had gotten herself a job at Southern Bell and was supporting herself and little Danny. And, she said, she wanted Kevin, her first and only true love, back in her life.

It was like getting a Dear John letter in reverse. Kevin was shocked at first, but he was also flattered and moved. He really had loved Betty, and hearing of her and her son's plight moved him. Above all else, Kevin's personality was motivated by the need to help others, and here was his one true love and her innocent child that needed him more than anyone else.

Kevin asked her if she was really off drugs. She assured him she was. He asked her if she could stay off drugs for the rest of her life. Betty promised him that she could and would. Kevin told her that he was willing to restart their relationship, but only under the condition that there were no drugs involved. "I'm going to be an army officer," he told her. "I can't have this around my family." Not only could she not take drugs, she could not associate with anyone who took drugs. Betty agreed.

They continued to correspond by phone and by mail. When Kevin graduated in June 1980, Betty made the trip up to New York State along with Kevin's family. Myron watched his son graduate from West Point. Kevin had made it into the top half of his graduating class—"but just barely," he recalled.

He'd done it. In less than four years, Kevin had gone from being sure he would be expelled and asking his father if he could quit and go home, to graduating from one of the toughest schools in the world. Kevin had gone from dumped ex-boyfriend to heroic knight in shining armor back to rescue his one true love and her little boy. And, to top it all off, he was what he always wanted to be—a second lieutenant in the United States Army, a squad leader, a leader of men.

The next day, Myron and Milre, Kevin's mother, and his brother and sister welcomed him home to their Pinecrest home. The rivalry between the Army, Navy and the Air Force had become less of a sore point and more of a source of good-natured ribbing.

But it was hardly blissful at the Pedersen household. Myron was drinking more heavily than ever, and—no longer able to abuse his now-grown children—he took out his frustrations on his wife, their mother. One evening that summer, he started slapping her around in front of Kevin, who had seen enough. Although trained as a wrestler, he knew how to throw a pretty good punch. A well-placed right cross sent his dad to the floor. The message was clear. That wasn't going to happen again. "The guilt afterwards was over-whelming," Kevin later said. "But it turned out to be the very last incident of him physically abusing her."

Kevin had a summer break before he had to report for active duty, and he spent as much as he could of it with Betty and little Danny—"making up for lost time," as he said.

He really took to the kid right away, later saying that he was more in love with Danny than Betty.

After a few days and a lot of thought, Kevin decided to propose marriage to her. He knew that Betty could get an uncontested divorce because her husband was behind bars doing time for trafficking.

Kevin didn't really have time for his old friends, and to the surprise of pretty much everyone, didn't meet up with Alex even once. He didn't even know where his old friend was, and nobody was really talking about him. If they did, they would be enigmatic about Alex or even downright evasive.

Kevin was too busy to worry, though. He had a fiancée and a new son to get to know and plans for their future together to make.

It seemed to everyone, not the least of which Kevin himself, that he had everything he ever wanted. But it wasn't going to last.

Betty had been true to her word, had kept off drugs and had cut out everybody in her life that used drugs. But she was working in her downtown Miami office on a sunny afternoon in August 1980 when someone came in to spray for bugs. Cockroaches are a major problem in hot, humid South Florida, and companies such as Southern Bell do their best to get rid of them as quickly as they can.

Unfortunately, the person they hired wasn't very good at his job and he had inadvertently mixed together two chemicals that reacted and created a toxic gas cloud. As he sprayed, employees quickly realized something had gone wrong. They expected bug spray to smell bad, but they were coughing and choking from the noxious stuff he used. Betty and everyone else was evacuated as the reeking ball of gas spread throughout the building.

Once outside, the other Southern Bell employees started to notice that Betty was not at all well. Once they had stopped coughing and returned to normal, they saw that she was acting erratically and talking without making any sense. Then she passed out. A coworker called an ambulance, and then called Kevin.

When she woke in a nearby hospital with Kevin at her bedside, he had to explain to her what had happened. The toxic gas had affected her more acutely than the others, and she had a severe vascular reaction that would be a problem for the rest of her life.

Southern Bell owned up to its responsibility to Betty, paid her medical bills, and put her on disability leave, sending her a check every two weeks.

Betty was at home, bored, depressed, and in constant pain. Finally, she could take it no longer. One day, when Kevin was busy with Danny, she snuck out of the house and went to a bar she used to frequent off US 1 near the Dadeland Mall. The bartender greeted her and told her that he knew she'd be back. She scored a little bit of weed from him. Her body desperately cried out for cocaine, but she was afraid to take any. She remembered what happened to her and her husband earlier, and she wanted to keep her promise to Kevin.

Once she had the joint in her hands, she just couldn't wait, and smoked up in the alley behind the bar.

As the weeks went by, her couple of harmless little joints became the occasional bump or line of coke. Just a couple of months after she had taken a solemn vow never to do drugs again, she was back on cocaine.

Kevin chalked up Betty's mood swings to her medical condition. Friends and family, including his brother Mike, tried to tell him that Betty was taking drugs again—as people who had lived in Miami during the drug tsunami of the late 1970s while Kevin was away at West Point, they could see the signs as plain as day.

But he wouldn't believe them. She was the love of his life, and he knew she would never break her promise to him. Years later, he would realize that turning a blind eye to her problem almost certainly made it worse, that he was enabling her drug use by not confronting her.

But he didn't know that at the time. There was just Betty, his first and only romance, who had been swept up in things beyond her control—Zalinsky's drug dealing, her own problems with drugs, the accidental poisoning with the bug spray—and all he wanted to do was help her, save her. And to make his desire to intervene even more profound, she had an innocent little baby. A child he had grown to love as well.

He made his mind up. Kevin proposed to Betty shortly after the summer break started. He offered to give her and little Danny his last name and all the love he had.

CHAPTER 5

Alex Went Up to Georgia

B ack in the mid-1970s, college athletic recruiting was nothing at like the refined, meticulous process it is now. If a prospect like Alex DeCubas was graduating from high school these days, coaches around the nation would not only have studied hours of video of his performances on the mat, they would have talked to him in person, and interviewed his parents, his coach and his teachers about his character, personality and will to take his game to the next level.

But it just wasn't that way back then. Instead, big-time coaches would send their assistants out to catch a match or two of kids in the region who they knew had good stats and records. Those assistants would then report back to the coach and tell him if they believed the kid appeared to have what it takes or not.

So, when an assistant came back to University of Georgia Hall of Fame wrestling coach George Reid raving and gushing over this heavyweight kid from suburban Miami, Reid offered Alex DeCubas a full-ride scholarship without even laying eyes on him.

He'd never seen Alex—live or on film. He couldn't pick him out of a crowd, although he would probably see him and figure that he was a wrestler, or at least should be. "I didn't know what I was getting, I knew he had a good record, he was two-time state champion," Reid later said. "When we started practicing, and I saw him wrestle, I realized that Alex was a good wrestler, pretty much almost instantly, and I said this kid's going to be pretty good . . . I've got a good find here."

He did indeed. Alex, as many people recollected, looked very strong, but was somehow much stronger than that. Reid was shocked by how much potential this thickly muscled incoming freshman had. Because it was more than just strength; he also brought with him a tenacity and a will to win, to dominate, that few could come close to, let alone match.

"On his feet, he was extremely hard to take down because he was so strong, his hips were so strong," Reid said. "On bottom, he was just about impossible to hold down, he'd just explode out of the bottom."

In fact, getting out of scrapes had become something of a specialty for Alex. If an opponent somehow managed to get Alex on the bottom, he would actually be less at an advantage because Alex was nearly impossible to contain and control in that position. He was so powerful from the bottom that his teammates gave up even trying to beat him. "I can remember many times, he'd call me over to wrestle him on top position," Reid said. "And he'd be down and I'd be on top position because most of the guys in the room couldn't ride him."

According to former Palmetto and Georgia teammate and long-time friend, Scott Sherouse, Alex could "deadlift six hundred, squat five hundred and bench press four-hundred, [with] the agility of a ballerina."

More important, though, was that he seemed not to care at all about getting hurt. Fear was for the other guy. Sherouse added that Alex "didn't seem to feel physical pain very much." It was almost as though God designed the perfect heavyweight wrestler.

He was a natural, but as a freshman, he still had a lot to learn about the sport. But he acquitted himself very well, not just on the mat, but also in the locker room. "He did whatever it was I asked of him as far as an athlete. He worked hard, he never missed practice, he was a leader here in the room, and kids looked up to him," Reid said. "That's the type of person he was, he wouldn't quit on you, no matter what the situation was. I had the greatest respect for what he did for me and what he did for the program."

Alex was far more successful than almost anyone could have predicted in his freshman year, going 10–3 in the regular season and placing third in his weight class at the 1977 SEC championships.

What makes that feat even more remarkable is that Alex managed to do that, pass his courses, and still be known as the biggest party animal on campus.

Emboldened by the knowledge that he could take down and keep down anyone else on campus or around town, Alex generally did as he pleased in Athens, often while drunk. The University of Georgia was a great place to be back then. Punk rock and disco were still running their courses, but a new kind of music, a little more intelligent with a little more emotion, but still lots of fun, was emerging. And with bands such as the B-52s and R.E.M. performing at places like the legendary 40 Watt Club, Athens had become something of a cultural capital. People came from all over the country and even from overseas to party there.

There are many stories about Alex's alcohol-fueled exploits through the town, but none is repeated more often than the time he stole the hog.

The University of Georgia's College of Agricultural and Environmental Sciences has a Department of Poultry Science, at which students learn about and research chickens, turkeys, and other agriculturally important birds and, sometimes, mammals.

The wrestlers had heard that they were experimenting with pig breeding at the department, and decided to pay it a nocturnal visit. Sherouse, who was Alex's teammate not just at Palmetto, but also at Georgia, recalls that members of the team started talking about the pigs, and Alex decided he wanted to have one. The boys had a trailer out in woods where they held parties and barbeques. He wanted, as teammate Brett Moses (now a mixed martial arts promoter) remembered, to get the biggest pig they had and roast it for all their friends.

Under the cover of darkness, they broke into the barn and opened the cage of the biggest hog. Alex went in, wrestled the 300-pound behemoth into submission, knocked it out cold, carried it out to the parking lot, and threw it into the trunk of a teammate's car.

About halfway to the trailer, though, the car started bouncing. The immense hog had suddenly regained consciousness, and was panicking in the claustrophobic darkness of the trunk.

Alex stopped the car, and the crew piled out. Alex opened the trunk and one of the other wrestlers shot the hog in the head with a handgun he had hidden in his jacket. It was a miracle he missed the car's gas tank.

When they finally got the dead monster back to the trailer, they were disappointed to realize they had forgotten to get any beer.

Alex knew what to do. There was a frat house not far away that always held massive parties. The wrestlers would just go and liberate one of their kegs. It was hardly the first time they'd lifted a keg from a frat, and they knew that if anyone had a problem with it, they could almost certainly take care of it.

Since it was a football weekend, the campus and surrounding area were alive with parties. Alex parked in front of the frat house they had targeted and told them his plan. Two of the smaller guys would pretend to get in a fight, roll around a little in the middle of the party, to create a diversion. Meanwhile, Alex and Moses would make off with one of their kegs and run it out to the car.

It worked, and the wrestlers also recruited many of the people at the frat to go party with them at the trailer with their beer and almost unlimited pork.

According to Sherouse and Moses, Alex pulled stuff like that all the time. The wrestling team was known on campus for rowdy, even frightening, behavior. And all of it, they say, originated with Alex.

Alex used to find odd things funny. Like, at night, drunk, he'd stand out front of a frat house and demand they send out their "biggest, baddest guy" just so he could beat him up in front of them.

But it wasn't always just pointless, nihilistic violence. Alex still had his protective instinct, and watched out for his guys. One of his friends, Grant Miller, was having a hard time with a drunk at an off-campus bar. The guy started threatening him. "Alex had no clue what was happening," Miller later recalled, "and he came over and—*bam!*—just cleaned the guy's clock."

Everybody on campus knew Alex. The football players—many of whom were on the school's 1980 national championship team— called him the "Crazy Cuban."

The two teams had a bit of a rivalry on campus, and Alex—in particular—had a problem with what he considered the preferential treatment the football team received. When he found a chalkboard with football plays drawn on it in the wrestling room, much to the delight of his wrestling teammates, destroyed it using nothing but repeated blows with his forehead.

That was Alex, he was up for anything, even if it was painful or dangerous—maybe particularly so. Sherouse recalled that the Georgia wrestlers were "four-wheeling" (driving off-road) when Alex took a Jeep through a veritable lake of muck at about thirty miles per hour. After about twenty feet, the Jeep got stuck and stopped suddenly. Alex's face smashed into the steering wheel with such force that his front teeth went right through his upper lip and were jutting out the other side. Alex suddenly threw the Jeep into reverse, backed up, and made a second run at the mud, faster this time, and made it all the way through, laughing and bleeding all the while.

But his behavior away from the mat didn't get him in any trouble. Not with Reid, certainly. Back then, "boys will be boys" was something of a mantra among college coaches. Athletes pulled stuff like that all the time and never had to worry about it. And Alex was no ordinary athlete. If he almost won the SEC title as a freshman, Reid couldn't imagine what he could do as a senior, junior, or even a sophomore. Alex made no secret of the fact that his goal was to represent the United States in the 1980 Olympics in Moscow, and Reid had little, if any, doubt that he could.

In his freshman year at Georgia—at the same time Kevin had to quit wrestling just to scrape by at West Point after his father denied his request to come home—Alex seemed to have it all. He was popular, he was feared, he was a star athlete headed for bigger things and, surprisingly, he was also a diligent student.

Alex had also found a calling away from the mat. He had always liked to design and build things, and had a natural talent for it also. In Athens, he could often be found in the school's metal shop, toiling away behind a lathe or welding something together. His long-range plan was to see how far wrestling would take him, and then study for his dream job as an architect. At the very least, he thought, he could always return to South Florida and get an industrial arts teaching job at a high school and maybe coach wrestling as well.

When he returned for his sophomore year at Georgia, Alex was the wrestling team's star attraction. Somehow, he was even stronger, tougher, and more competitive than ever before. As was becoming the DeCubas family tradition, all eyes were on Alex, and he thoroughly enjoyed it.

He had even become something of a recruiter for the Bulldogs, convincing Andrew DeWitt, who was a year behind him at Palmetto, and Robert Moses, who was also from the Miami area, to accept scholarship offers from Georgia.

Alex was so powerful that he had a hard time getting the other Georgia wrestlers to even practice with him. But there was one drill that everyone enjoyed taking part in, in no small measure because they all got to take their shots at Alex. Most schools call it King of the Hill; but at Georgia, it was called Bull in the Ring. In the drill, one wrestler tries to defend the center of the mat against all comers. Success is determined by how long the bull can hold the ring as his own territory.

"We have everyone out there, and one guy in the ring," said Reid. "The idea is that we give you a fresh body, to try to wear you out." It's a great teaching tool because it forces wrestlers to rely more heavily on discipline, technique, and ingenuity as fatigue saps their strength and reflexes.

Of course, Alex—with his naturally thick and powerful lower body and ability to make split-second decisions—dominated.

Reid liked having Alex as the Bull because it made him a smarter, more disciplined wrestler, and it forced the other wrestlers to get better. Alex loved being the bull because it made him the big man, the one to be acknowledged as the best—if not downright feared. The other guys liked the drill because it would pit them against the best and actually give them a chance to beat Alex as he tired after taking on everyone else, often twice.

It was during one of these Bull in the Ring drills—early in his sophomore year, before the regular season began—that Alex was, as usual, dominating.

Everybody knows that the best way to bring down a bigger opponent is to go low, and Alex was no different. It was a tough task—because of his thick hips and thighs—but it was the only way to get it done.

So, when one of the other Bulldogs came in at the bull low in a takedown attempt, Alex was ready. He planted and pivoted in an instant, readying his body for the assault.

Then it happened. Everyone in the gym heard the sickening pop, followed by the big man going down untouched and bellowing on the mat, clearly in intense pain.

Alex had timed his move perfectly, but his toes got caught in the seam between two mats and stuck. When he twisted his knee to meet his opponent, his shin, ankle, and foot, stuck in the mats, didn't make the trip. The resulting torsion tore his meniscus—that vital little piece of cartilage that keeps the femur from rubbing against the tibia—to shreds.

Alex had to put his wrestling dreams on hold. The chance at SEC and potential national championships would have to wait until after he healed. Until then, he could rehab, concentrate on his studies, and just be Alex.

The partying didn't stop, or even slow down, though. Then-freshman DeWitt recalls going over to the house Alex lived in because he heard there was going to be a party there. When he arrived, he noticed that Alex had already had a few drinks. The phone rang, and some other housemate picked it up. "Alex, it's your uncle," he shouted over the music. "He wants to talk to you."

Alex growled back that he didn't want to talk with him and went back to drinking and partying with his pals.

Somewhat later—at about 9:30 or 10, DeWitt recalls—one of the revelers ran up to Alex and told him that his uncle had called again, wanting to talk to him.

"Fuck him," Alex said. "I'm not in the mood for that."

He and his boys went back to drinking but maybe an hour after that, another guy came running up to Alex, who was outside, and told him that his uncle had called again.

DeWitt recalls that Alex went "stone-faced" and the "he looked completely sober." They all knew something important was going down.

Alex ran into the house and picked up the phone. The guys heard him speaking excitedly in Spanish. It was his uncle Pedro—the one who Castro had thrown in jail, but who had later made it to South Florida.

Pedro told Alex that Luis Senior had fallen very, very ill and that Alex had to get on the next flight to Miami to visit him in the hospital.

The very idea of mighty Luis being sick just did not compute in Alex's head. The very idea was preposterous. But he knew from the tone of Pedro's voice and from the fact that Luis would only go to the hospital if he absolutely had to, that the situation was dire.

Moments after he hung up, Alex—too much into his own thoughts to speak—jumped into his car and started in on his long, lonely ninety-minute drive to the airport.

Alex took the next plane to Miami, and Pedro met him at the airport. They didn't say much to one another on the ride down US 1 back to Pinecrest. But as Pedro passed by the hospital that he said Luis was in, Alex asked why they weren't taking the exit.

Pedro remained silent.

"I thought you said he was in the hospital," Alex pushed.

After another long pause, Pedro realized he could not avoid the question any longer. "Your father's dead, Alex."

*   *   *

Luis Junior, who had been living with his parents and working at the family store, was at home with Nena when two police officers knocked on the door. They told them the news. At a little before noon, Luis had gone into the Don Luis office, locked the door behind him and shot himself in the chest. Always the showman, he used a Walther PPK, the same gun James Bond always carried. Luis bled out before anyone could get into the room.

Upon hearing the news, Luis Junior and Nena sped to Coral Gables. But the police, who still surrounded the scene, would not let them inside.

They had returned home by the time Alex and Pedro arrived. In fact, when they got there, the house was packed. Along with Luis's friends and relatives, there were people like Zimbler and Sherouse there to help support Alex (Kevin was still at West Point, and couldn't come down).

But it wasn't the rollicking good time people usually had at the DeCubas house with Nena making sure everyone had too much to eat while Alex and his friends snuck a few beers. It was incredibly somber. Luis was not just a husband and father; he was a larger-than-life figure. He was a hero. After all, he had fled the communists with just five lousy bucks in his pocket to become a rich and respectable man.

But that was the problem. Luis wasn't really rich. Don Luis had fallen on hard times, the sales just weren't there. In a fashion world skewing increasingly into the tastes of younger people who were influenced by disco, punk rock, and new wave, the gentlemanly suits he sold were severely out of style. Nobody wanted them anymore.

Debts were mounting, and creditors were hounding Luis day and night. For him, life was all about the respect you got—respect for taking care of your family, respect for earning your own way in life, and respect for being scrupulously honest.

He just didn't have that anymore. For Luis, the shame and sadness of closing Don Luis, or even worse, the horrors of bankruptcy, were far worse than taking a bullet to the heart and ending it all.

The following morning, Alex and Luis Junior went out to the store. They needed answers. They needed to know why their dad had shot himself and—as crazy as it sounds—their confused, grieving brains needed to know that he was dead. He had always seemed invincible to them.

There was no doubt when they got there. The police had taken all kinds of evidence, but the blood was still there. Luis had been a big man, and it seemed like every drop of blood that had run through his veins was now on the floor of the shop.

It hit the boys hard, especially Alex, who had always been his father's darling and was also a very emotional person. "When Alex and I saw the blood, we were both cleaning it, he was sobbing really bad and crying, I was crying, but he was really down on the floor crying," recalled Luis Junior. "He was in a bad situation."

Luis's boys did what he would have in the same situation—they went to work. Alex and Luis Junior got down on their hands and knees to scrub the shop clean. Deep in a pool of his dead father's blood, Alex wept and wailed. He was mourning not just a man, but an institution, a legend, a way of life and pretty much everything he had ever believed in—taken away from him in one shot.

Alex came home, his clothes, shoes, arms, legs, and even his face all stained with his father's blood. Still just twenty years old, he had no idea why his father shot himself. Why, he asked himself, would he tear apart his family like that? Everything seemed so perfect, why would he want to end it?

Nena had the answer. After he showered and changed, she handed Alex and Luis Junior each an envelope. Inside were letters from their father. Luis, always the gentleman, had taken the time to write individual suicide notes to every member of his family. They all had their names on the outside of the envelope except for the one meant for Alex, that was addressed, of course, to El Tigre. It began:

To Alex, my beloved son the Tiger,
Do not let anybody make you think I was a coward because
I took my own life, because believe me, my beloved son, it

takes more courage to pull a trigger against yourself than face
people not respecting you because you owe them money. I will
be watching you from Heaven, protecting you not to be hurt.

The suicide notes all followed the same templates, although each
was personalized and Alex's was the longest—four pages—and the
most emotional.

The gist of the letters was that Luis had worked so hard because
he had wanted to provide for his kids, he sent them to the best
schools, gave them the best food and clothes and even cars when
they were old enough. But he wouldn't be able to do that once his
creditors came to get him. He simply had too much pride, he admitted, to allow his family to have that happen to them. Killing himself, he maintained, was the best solution for everyone. He honestly
believed in his heart of hearts that his suicide was the best thing he
could do for his kids; he thought it would make their lives easier.

But Alex's letter had a little extra. Alongside the rationalization of
his suicide, he had some advice for his favorite son. Luis compelled
Alex to get all he could out of life, to be successful because, in the
end, nothing else mattered. "You've made me so proud, my tiger," it
read. "Now go be a success. Go out and grab life with gusto."

After his father's death, friends noticed Alex had changed profoundly. He was quieter, more serious, less spontaneous, less fun.
He was still Alex, but he wasn't really the Alex they had known
before.

In the early stages of grief, he was absent, going about his daily
routine in a zombie-like state of detachment. Finally, Nena convinced Alex to go back to Georgia, finish his degree and keep on
wrestling after his knee got better—using the old "he would have
wanted it this way" tactic was the capper. Luis Junior would take
over the store, or arrange to sell it. Alex agreed to do exactly what
his mother suggested.

Back in Athens, all his friends, housemates, and teammates did their best to help out their injured friend. But one friend was particularly willing to lend a hand—and certainly felt as though he had to. Back at Palmetto, DeWitt was a year behind Alex and wrestled in the same weight class. That meant for two years at Palmetto and another at Georgia, DeWitt wrestled Alex essentially every day. That can make sure a couple of guys get to know each other.

And in 1976, when he was a junior, DeWitt lost his own father. He just disappeared one day. Years later, police would find out that some men he owed money took him on a boat ride, killed him, and dumped his body in the Atlantic Ocean; but, for years, DeWitt's dad was just missing, and he had hopes that he would return one day.

One of the things that helped him get through it was Alex. Always ready with a hug or kind word, Alex helped give DeWitt the strength to carry on, even though they had never been the closest of friends.

DeWitt thought he could return the favor. But it wouldn't be easy. Alex returned to Georgia a very different person, one unwilling to talk in depth about what happened at Don Luis.

After a few weeks, Alex finally couldn't hold it in anymore. Surrounded by close friends in the Athens house, he began to break down. Sympathetically, DeWitt told him, "Let it out of you, man. It's OK." Although he was weeping profusely, Alex still did not want to talk about his father. Instead, he asked DeWitt and another teammate to shave his head. They did.

Even though his knee had not yet completely healed, Alex went back into competition. He wasn't the same Alex anymore. And it was not just his knee. His technique was off; his famed decision-making ability was shot. "He looked tight out there. He didn't look good," recalled DeWitt. "I had never seen Alex not look good before." He began to lose, even get pinned. "He lost a few that he wouldn't have if he was still the focused, committed athlete he was before," DeWitt said.

And his after-hours shenanigans changed as well. While he used to be out there and sometimes violent, his stunts were always about bonding the team, keeping them unified as a group. But after his father's suicide, they became a lot less about the team, and more violent. Fewer and fewer of them would be willing to go out with Alex at night. It just wasn't fun anymore.

He was a different person. His drive and confidence were shot. Alex wasn't the wrestler he had been, or the bon vivant. His studies suffered. He started skipping classes regularly and drinking more. Things weren't working out in the house with his teammates. Alex moved out, and took up residence, alone with himself and his thoughts, in a trailer down by the Oconee River.

There was, however, one guy he always stayed in touch with regularly—Scott Sherouse. A little older than Alex, he had been something of a bad boy at Palmetto High, and was well known for finding his own path.

After leaving school, he had managed to get a job repairing small boats at the Atlantic Undersea Test and Evaluation Center (AUTEC), a US Navy facility on Andros Island in the Bahamas. Although security was extremely high at the base—they tested nuclear submarines there, after all—the island itself was a notorious transit point for drug traffickers.

The Bahamas made perfect sense for smugglers, who had used it for moving product since the old colonial days. It's a sprawling archipelago made up of about 700 islands, many of them uninhabited, spread over more than 180,000 square miles. It's not far from South America, and its closest island, North Bimini, is just about fifty-five miles from Florida. Since smuggling had been going on there since the pirate days and was an easy way to make serious money, many in the nation had a relaxed attitude towards it. At least back then, elected officials, judges, and cops could easily be persuaded to turn a blind eye to any minor illegality as long as there would be a few bucks in it for them.

Sherouse was in Andros Town one night in 1978 when he started talking to a man in a bar. They had a few laughs about how there were plenty of people moving tons of marijuana just a few feet away from some of the tightest security in the world. "You know," the guy told him. "Some of the weed goes missing from time to time."

Intrigued, Sherouse asked him to elaborate.

The guy told him he could get him a thousand pounds of it if he wanted.

Intrigued, Sherouse asked him how much it would cost.

The guy told him thirty bucks a pound.

If this was a cartoon, Sherouse would have had dollars signs in his eyes. Sherouse had never sold weed before, but he knew that thirty bucks was ridiculously low. He knew people who sold weed for a lot more than that. If he could get the stuff to Florida, he thought, he'd have no problem getting rid of it.

Sherouse bought it, borrowed a friend's boat and sailed for Miami. He asked around town and quickly found a buyer. The guy would pay $330 a pound. Then a friend told him his cousin in North Dakota would pay $380 a pound.

Sherouse didn't have to be told twice. He packed up as much as he could fit in his luggage, and booked a flight to North Dakota. Security on domestic flights back then was almost nonexistent, but Sherouse was nervous anyway. When some turbulence caused his overhead package to slam against the inside of the compartment, filling the plane with the unmistakable scent of weed, he was sure he was going to jail. But he was wrong. There was no problem getting it off and passing it through security.

Of course, his buyer wanted the weed, all of it and any more he could get his hands on.

For an investment of $3,000 and a roundtrip flight north, Sherouse had made more than $35,000. "I thought I was a millionaire," he said.

When he came back to Andros Island, Sherouse didn't think of himself as a drug dealer. He was just a guy who did a little weekend thing that made him more than a year's salary with very little effort. And, he had to admit, the fear of getting caught actually made the whole thing pretty exciting.

It was so exciting, in fact, that he felt like he had to tell someone—It was Alex, of course. Although he was still mourning, Alex told his old friend that he was happy for him, and impressed he had been able to pull it off. Although he loved to drink, Alex was—in principle, at least—against drugs. He wasn't in the way of anyone else having a good time; it just wasn't his thing.

When the opportunity to do it again emerged, Sherouse jumped at the chance. Before long, he had transformed himself from a humble boat mechanic to a big-time trafficker.

When Alex came home for spring break, just six months after Luis had killed himself, Sherouse dropped by to see if he couldn't help his old friend get through the grieving process. He also wanted to show off his expensive new clothes and his recently purchased Mercedes-Benz.

What he saw there broke his heart. Not only was the DeCubas family still mourning Luis, but his suicide had not saved them, as Luis had hoped, from financial difficulty. They could lose the house and Alex might have to leave college, he thought.

So Sherouse made a decision. He had to help his old friend and his family. He asked Alex if he could do him a favor. Alex said of course, without asking him what it was. Sherouse took him out to the garage at his place and asked him to pick up a big, rectangular package wrapped in plastic and put it in his trunk. It was, of course, no problem for mighty Alex.

Sherouse then told him they needed to take a ride. Alex agreed, and came with him to a house he'd never seen before. When they arrived, Sherouse asked Alex to take the package out of the trunk and give it to the guy in the house. Again, Alex agreed without question.

The task done, Alex got back in the car. Sherouse smiled at him, and took a roll of bills out of his front pocket. "Take it, you've earned it," he said, passing the cash to Alex.

Alex, confused, took the $1,500.

On the way back, Sherouse laid out a plan for Alex, who already knew his old friend was making stacks of cash moving marijuana. They had been talking frequently since Luis had died and one of the things Sherouse had found out was that, since Alex was from Miami, a lot of people in Georgia (mostly football players and other athletes) had been approaching him looking to see if they could score some weed from him. The city had that kind of reputation.

Alex and Sherouse agreed that selling weed at the University of Georgia would not only be simple and profitable, but—because Alex was Alex—he wouldn't have to worry about getting ripped off or leaned on by other dealers. He just didn't know how to get any.

Sherouse did, of course. One of the idiosyncrasies about AUTEC was that when they collected the mail back to the United States, they didn't look at any of it. Nothing was searched, X-rayed or sniffed at all. Navy men could be shipping plutonium back home, and Uncle Sam would be none the wiser.

Sherouse was already sending weed back home for others to sell, so why not Alex as well?

He assured him it wouldn't be a big deal, just a few pounds every now and then—just enough to keep him in college and maybe help the family out a little bit.

It never would have happened if Luis was alive, but by the spring of 1978, Alex wasn't trying to get anyone's respect anymore.

And he needed the money. Seconds after Sherouse had made the offer, Alex smiled broadly and shook his hand.

CHAPTER 6

War in South Florida

July is just too hot and humid in Miami for tourists to want to visit. They never go too far away from the beach anyway, unless they are headed to the Everglades or somewhere like that. So, the Dadeland Mall in 1979 was the kind of place where you would see real Miami, away from what you'd see in travel brochures, as it was back then.

About two miles north of Pinecrest, the Dadeland Mall was one of America's first enclosed shopping centers when it was built in 1962. It was immediately popular—especially in the summer months when Miamians wanted someone else to pay for the air conditioning—and it grew rapidly. It was extremely popular, becoming so synonymous with shopping in the area that most people for miles around just called it "the mall" because everybody knew which one they meant.

It was a blistering Wednesday afternoon in July 1979, and nobody really paid too much attention to the brand-new white Ford cube van as it was awkwardly backed into a parking spot. It looked like any other commercial delivery truck, except it had "Happy Time

Complete Party Supply 6648275" painted in red on the left side and "Happy Time Complete Supply Party 6648275" on the right.

About a half hour later, a brand-new white Mercedes-Benz sedan pulled up and parked a few feet away from the cube van. The two men who had been inside the car headed to the outside entrance of Crown Liquors, tucked between Mr. John's beauty salon on the left and a Cozzoli's Pizza & Deli outlet on the right.

Both of the men were Latino, but that drew nobody's attention because Miami was experiencing a boom in its Spanish-speaking population by then.

One of the guys, the older one, was wearing expensive tan pants and a tailored pale blue shirt, and was regular sized. But the other one, in jeans and a cheap blue shirt, was big. Not big like Alex, but big, and very strong looking.

Once they were inside the store, the smaller guy, clearly the more important one, in heavily accented English, asked Tom Capozzi, the man behind the counter, where the Chivas Regal was. Capozzi barely looked up, motioned to the wall on his right and said: "Over there." He knew the guys. Not their names or anything about them, really, just that they came into the store about this time every week to stock up on booze. They'd bought Chivas Regal before, but he and the stock boy had just rearranged a few things, and it was no longer in the place that they were used to it being. They never said much, and judging from their accents, Capozzi figured they didn't know all that much English anyway.

Just as the bigger guy turned to find his bottles of whiskey, Capozzi heard the rapid opening of a metal roller door and some-one yelling in Spanish. He looked up to see the back door of the white cube van—which was facing the store—wide open and two armed men bursting out.

They ran into the store with their weapons drawn. One of them had a Beretta .380-caliber semiautomatic handgun. He walked up to the smaller customer and shot him four times in the face. The other intruder was armed with an Ingram Mac-10 submachine gun, also with a silencer, and he shot at everything in the store other than his partner. The thunderous shower of hot metal destroyed just about everything in the store, except for the men shooting. After their initial volley, they both replaced their clips, and shot at anything they thought might still be alive.

The two customers lay dead on the floor—the smaller one missing big chunks of his head—blood rapidly mixing with various liquors over broken glass.

Capozzi, thinking it was a robbery, had quickly taken cover behind the counter, but had been hit in the shoulder. The bullet struck him with such force that it actually exited through his chest, tearing at bone, ligament, muscle, and even his lungs on its transit through his body. The gunman figured him for dead or close to it, even as he crawled past them on his hands and knees toward the door.

The initial sounds of violence drew the curiosity of Morgan Perkins, an eighteen-year-old stock boy who had been eating his lunch in the back room. He emerged as the assailants were reloading a second time, and realizing the danger he was in, fell to the floor, crawled his way out the entrance and ran, finally diving under a parked car for cover.

The crowd at Cozolli's—mostly an older bunch—heard the noise (silencers are nowhere near as effective in real life as they are in the movies), but didn't know what it was. Most probably wrote it off as construction, and one witty fellow shouted: "Skylab is falling!"—a reference to the pioneering space station that did indeed fall to Earth later that day in Australia.

While the other customers were chuckling, a woman and her young son left and went into the parking lot. First, they saw the broken glass and then they could see Capozzi, struggling and barely alive, in an increasingly large pool of his own blood.

Frightened, they ran back to the deli. But—suddenly aware of the situation—the people inside had locked the front doors seconds earlier. The woman and her boy pounded on the glass doors helplessly, shouting "They're shooting! Call the police!" and "Somebody's hit in the parking lot!"

But the people in Cozolli's wouldn't budge from their hiding spots. Frustrated and afraid but in control, the brave woman told her son to run to their car (which was actually unlocked) and she ran into Mr. John's on the other side of Crown Liquors.

The staff and customers there had heard the noise, but all decided it was probably just kids lighting off some firecrackers. After seeing and hearing the woman who ran in, the manager called 911.

As all of that was happening, the shooters walked calmly into the cab of the Party Time van—a driver was waiting for them—and started to drive away. One of them spotted Perkins in his hiding spot and opened fire. "Why are they shooting at me?" he later recalled screaming to his assailants in the van. "I didn't do anything." He took bullets to both feet.

Speeding through the parking lot to the southern exit of the mall, they kept firing indiscriminately, taking out plate glass windows and putting hundreds of holes in dozens of cars. One car took a shell right in the fuel tank, flooding much of the parking lot with gallons of easily combustible gasoline. Shoppers were fleeing, screaming, desperately trying to avoid the hail of bullets surrounding them. The men were shooting so chaotically, they managed to take out their own right side mirror.

The two Crown Liquor customers were dead—both Capozzi and Perkins survived, nobody else was hit—and Dadeland Mall looked like a combat zone. The entire attack—from rolling up the cube van's back door to escaping on the highway—took less than three minutes.

The 911 call from Mr. John's reached the Miami-Dade County

Public Safety Department at 2:35 p.m., just as the assailants were tearing out of the parking lot.

Dozens of police cars, ambulances, and the fire department's hazardous materials team showed up within minutes. The bad guys were long gone, but there was evidence to collect, witnesses to interview, a huge gas spill to contain, victims to rescue, and two bodies to bring to the morgue.

As soon as Miami-Dade homicide detective Al Singleton was informed, his heart sank. Just from the barest description of the Dadeland Mall shooting he already pieced together what had happened, and why. In the previous eight months, twenty-four Latino men had been murdered in Miami. Every single one of those shootings had left behind victims who were intimately involved with the drug trade, but also left very little in the way of useful evidence. Singleton, an ex-Marine, figured the Dadeland Mall incident was another one of them, and there would be more.

He was right. The two men who had been assassinated at Crown Liquors were German Jimenez Panesso—a thirty-seven-year-old *jefe*, or chief, in one of the local cocaine dealing organizations— and the big guy was Juan Carlos Hernandez, his twenty-two-year-old bodyguard. Their bodies were in rough shape. Not only was Jimenez Panesso missing significant parts of his head, a medical examiner told the *Miami Herald*: "They looked like Swiss cheese." Someone was clearly sending a message.

Police found a loaded nine-millimeter Browning semiautomatic pistol in the backseat of their Mercedes, but they clearly thought it would be fine to make a five-minute stop at a liquor store in Miami's busiest mall in broad daylight on a Wednesday afternoon with it still in the car.

It wasn't. Cocaine had changed Miami. And Jimenez Panesso had made the dumbest, most basic, of all gangster mistakes—he kept a set schedule. If Capozzi knew they would be coming in at about that time, so did anyone who had watched them for a while.

Jimenez Panesso had made the wrong enemy. Back in April of 1978, a small-time dealer named Jaime Suescun burglarized Jimenez Panesso's Miami house, stole two kilos of coke and, when his housekeeper, Ester Rios, caught him in the act, he strangled her to death.

Jimenez Panesso found out who had done the job when Suescun started hitting the nightclubs the following night telling everyone in Miami that he had come across two kilos of cocaine and needed to unload it quickly.

A couple of days later, Suescun was told that some guys, new on the scene straight out of Colombia, had a couple of kilos they were willing to let go for the ridiculously low price of $16,000 each. Suescun jumped at the chance and agreed to meet them.

A week after Jimenez Panesso's coke was stolen and Rios was murdered, Suescun's body was found in the trunk of an Audi surrounded by bags of icing sugar packaged to look like cocaine.

It was bold, it was brash, and it was a huge mistake. Jimenez Panesso had made another fundamental error. The Audi that Suescun's body was found in was registered to his name. The cops couldn't do anything about it, but Suescun's people sure could.

He happened to work for a guy who worked for a guy who worked for the notorious Griselda "La Madrina" (the Godmother) Blanco Restrepo. She would later be accused of more than 200 murders, including that of a four-year-old boy and three of her former husbands. She was not someone you'd want to cross.

When she found out that it was a car registered to Jimenez Panesso that her soldier had been found in, his fate was sealed. It's not clear as to whether she knew about the rip (as the increasingly common thefts from dealers were called), or that Suescun was responsible for the death of Rios or not, but it's unlikely it would have mattered to her. That was how the cartels played—you killed my guy, so you have to die. It's just business, you understand.

The cops later found the Happy Time van abandoned on a country road. It was brand-new with just 108 miles on it. It had been equipped with armor plating that was put in after the purchase; and inside, the cops found plenty of weapons—submachine guns, semiautomatic pistols, sawed-off shotguns and ammo for all of them. They had more and better weapons than the police and vehicles that could stand up to anything the cops could throw at them. Even if the cops had arrived while the cube van was still at the mall, there was not much they could have done about it. The cocaine traffickers weren't just fighting each other anymore; they were prepared to fight law enforcement.

But finding the van didn't help the police all that much. The guys who did the shooting were pros, veterans of the savage conflict in Colombia, and they knew how to leave as little usable evidence as possible behind.

They tracked down the dealer who sold the truck. He told them the guy who bought it paid $14,000 cash. Paying with cash back then meant no identification was necessary. The salesman at the dealership gave a vague description of the buyer, but it didn't matter, the cops knew, because it was probably a straw buyer who put an innocent face on for the dealer and then flipped the truck to its real owner.

The party supply company—by either name—was, of course, fictitious, and calls to the phone number went to a disconnected line.

All of that made the Dadeland Mall shootings profoundly shocking for South Florida. The slickness of it all, the fact that the chance of the assassins ever getting caught was infinitesimally small, the number and sophistication of the weapons they used, and the chilling fact that they opened fire on innocent civilians made people in the area feel helpless. What could the police with their puny revolvers do to help them? The people of South Florida were living in a war zone, and everybody knew it.

Miami was at war because there was just so much money to be made in cocaine. The cartels had already made Colombia one of the most violent countries in the world, rendering its government impotent while gunfights and bombings killed thousands throughout the country.

Forget the cops, even our homegrown gangsters were no match for these guys. In New York, they did the smart thing. The Mafia families there negotiated a deal that left the cocaine market to the Colombians, providing manpower and intelligence for a small part of the revenue—but even a tiny slice of that pie would make many people fabulously wealthy.

But in Miami, they were stubborn. The old guard talked tough and vowed to stand firm. They were quickly, and ruthlessly, eliminated.

And, after they were gone, things got even more violent. The first set of Colombians made so much money that more Colombians came, willing to kill their way into the business. The escalation of both the money and the violence verged on the ridiculous.

The city, which had been used to a couple of dozen homicides per year, set a record with 249 in 1978, upped it to 573 in 1980 and hit 621 in 1981. It got so bad in the summer of 1981 that the city had to spend $800 a month to lease a refrigerated truck from the Burger King corporate headquarters, across the street from the Dadeland Mall, because the morgue couldn't accommodate all the bodies that were piling up. They didn't give the truck up until 1989, when a new morgue was built.

Arthur Patten, a local entrepreneur, told a reporter from *Time* magazine at the time that "I've been through two wars and no combat zone is as dangerous as Dade County."

It was no longer the Miami Kevin and Alex had grown up in.

* * *

Alex went back to Athens after spring break a different person. Once he healed enough, he went back on the mat. He wasn't bad—going 7–3–1 as a sophomore—but he didn't look like a champion anymore. After the season, he went to Coach Reid's office and quit the wrestling team.

Reid was disappointed, but understood. "He lost an awful lot when he lost his father," he said.

Alex went to class only occasionally after that, instead concentrating on selling weed and getting drunk. His high school girlfriend, Amy Doddridge, moved to Athens to help him out, to give him a feeling of normalcy.

As school finished, Alex returned to Miami. If he wasn't wrestling, he'd have to pay to go back to Athens—but how could he? Not by selling dime bags of weed for Scott Sherouse, that's for sure.

But he had friends. Ever the charmer, Alex was still very popular, and many people reached out to try to help him. One of them was Andrew DeWitt. He wanted to help Alex as much as Sherouse did, but he had a legal option.

His cousins owned the DeWitt Tool Co., an industrial supplier that specialized in drill bits and other cutting tools, primarily for the region's burgeoning aircraft repair and maintenance market. The store was a half-hour's drive north from Pinecrest, up by Hialeah, and it suited Alex's interest in things mechanical. Even if he didn't want to make it his life's work, it would pay enough for him to take care of his mother and maybe to go back to college. It wasn't a ton of money—about $9,400 a year, which would be about $32,000 in 2017 dollars—but at least it was something.

In June 1979, just before the Dadeland incident, he was hired by the DeWitt Tool Co., and installed at the front counter of the business, which everyone called DTC, greeting customers, filling orders, and answering phones.

He liked it. Alex quickly became familiar with all the tools and the processes that required them, he liked dealing with the customers and, since he spoke Spanish fluently, he increased the customer pool. It quickly became obvious to everyone that he wasn't going back to Athens—his dreams of being an architect or even a teacher were put on hold, at least for now.

But something wasn't quite right about the scenario. Alex knew in his heart of hearts that he wasn't just some low-income nine-to-five flunky, he was something special. His dad was right, Alex came around to thinking, being a success was everything. And it was essential that everyone around you knew that you were a success.

The Miami Alex came back to was not the one he left back in 1977. Back then, a Camaro was a fancy car. By the summer of 1979, his half-hour's drive up to work took him past dozens of Mercedes, Porsches, Ferraris and even the odd Lamborghini. Most guys were dressed to the nines, all day, every day. Armani and Versace had replaced Wrangler and Levi's. Beer and pig roasts were for backwoods hillbillies. In Miami, they drank champagne and fine, aged whiskeys with stone crab and lobster. Alex was clearly being left behind and falling into that amorphous mass of ordinary people.

He couldn't tolerate that, so he did a few things to make himself feel special. He didn't make a lot of money—weed prices had bottomed out in Miami after cocaine came to town—but he needed a car.

The smart thing to do probably would have been to drop by a Honda dealer and pick up a Civic or something similar. But that's what nobodies do. Alex had a different path ahead of him. For the same amount of money, he bought a 1966 Porsche 911. It was in rough shape—it had holes in the floorboards and the engine bay sounded like there was a woodpecker inside trying to escape—but it looked pretty damn good. He might be the counter person at a tool company, but at least he drove a Porsche.

And he dressed a little more like a player than you'd expect someone who answered the phone for a tool company. The DTC's owners, the Barnetts, must have noticed, but just laughed it off as Alex being Alex.

Later that summer, Alex was at the front counter when he saw a huge, caramel-colored Mercedes-Benz 450SEL pull up. The guy who came out of it was wearing a flashy Armani suit and he had gold everywhere. Alex was immediately impressed by the outsized Rolex Presidential he had on his right wrist.

The guy came in and asked Alex, in a heavy Eastern European accent, who he was. Alex introduced himself as the new guy, and asked if he could help him.

The friendly and expensively dressed customer was a Czech immigrant named Jaromir John, but everybody called him Jeremiah or, more often, JJ. He explained to Alex that he and his partner, Sam, had a jewelry-making business in the area and they came to DTC for machine parts when they needed them.

In a story that reminded Alex of his own father, John told him that had fled communist Czechoslovakia without a penny to his name. But he wasn't just dreaming of the freedom only America could provide, he was an active participant in the 1968 anti-communist uprising in Prague, throwing Molotov cocktails at Soviet trucks and soldiers. After the rebellion was quashed, John knew that he had to get out of Czechoslovakia. In 1971, he made it to New York. He'd been a jewelry maker in Prague, and quickly found work. But New York was crowded, expensive, and full of small-time criminals, so he chased his dream to Florida, where he set up shop and very quickly prospered.

The two men hit it off, and John seemed very interested in the fact that Alex spoke Spanish so well. He later described his first

impression of Alex was as a "friendly and intelligent person." After
a few minutes of joking around, John asked Alex if he would like a
line of cocaine. Alex jumped at the chance.

John grinned and told him "if you help me out on this machine
shop business, I can help you out with a little bit of coke."

Alex was intrigued. John set up a meeting with him at his work-
shop up in Fort Lauderdale. When Alex arrived, John introduced
him to Sam Frontera. Although he was John's partner, Frontera was
no jeweler; and he didn't even pretend to be. Instead, he told Alex
that he was an entertainment promoter who handled nightclubs
and musical acts. He did actually do that, but his primary source
of income came from being a small-time career criminal and drug
dealer—Boca Raton Detective and DEA Task Force member James
Burke described him as a "street thug." He started out in his native
Detroit, but had heard there was a lot of easy money to be made in
South Florida once cocaine had arrived there. Soon after he showed
up in Miami, he hooked up with John, and the two had a thriving
friendship and trafficking business.

Almost anyone looking at the pair would assume they were
criminals. John had the twitchy, too-serious look of a psycho (you
know, those guys who laugh when nothing's funny, but don't
when something really is), and Frontera gave off the vibe of an
old-school big-city badass you wouldn't want to mess with. But to
Alex, they just looked like good guys who could help him make
some money.

The told him they could get him as much coke as he could sell.
Alex told them he would see what he could do, and left with the
hope that he could figure out a way to sell it. He certainly wanted
to make big money, but he just didn't have a network for that kind
of thing. John told him he could unload it to his "Cuban boys," but
that wasn't Alex's crowd. He knew college students, tool salesmen,
and airplane mechanics. He didn't know any cocaine buyers.

But he knew someone who might. Alex drove over to Sherouse's house and told him about the opportunity that had opened up for him. He was right, Sherouse did know someone. He had a pal, Rick Olson (another former Palmetto High wrestler), who was, by the standards that Alex and Sherouse knew about at least, a big-time cocaine dealer. Alex had been introduced to him while he was still in college, and they'd hung out a bit. Sherouse tells a story about how Alex, exhausted after driving down from Athens, fell asleep on his couch after a few beers. For laughs, Sherouse and Olson blew marijuana smoke into Alex's face until they were sure he was high. When Alex woke up and said that he was hungry, they fell apart laughing.

After discussing the situation, Alex and Sherouse hopped into Sherouse's car. On the way to Olson's place near the airport— Sherouse told Alex about how he'd seen Miami Dolphins star half-back Eugene "Mercury" Morris there one time, and a little while later no less a star than Rolling Stones guitarist Ronnie Wood was sitting on Olson's coach like it was no big deal.

When they got there, Olson was delighted to see them. Of course, he wanted their coke, every single grain they could get their hands on. The stuff was white hot. Kilos were selling for $50,000 and when cut with additive and sold in individual hits, the revenue stream was exponentially deeper. And all of his people wanted more all the time.

In South Florida at the time, there was only one source of cocaine—the Colombians. It might have been grown in Peru or Bolivia, but it was processed in Colombia and transported north by Colombians. If you didn't want to play by their rules, you didn't get their coke—unless you were John and Frontera. Unlike every other coke dealer in South Florida, they didn't have any Colombian connections. They had a less conventional business model—they robbed other dealers.

To them, it made perfect sense. Besides the drugs, dealers usually had piles of cash lying around, and sometimes you might be able to pick up a nice watch or a gun. The guy you robbed was the one who had to face the Colombians when he couldn't deliver. For tough guys like John and Frontera, it was almost too easy.

Frontera once laughed at Sherouse for making a mere ten percent on his deals, saying, "I make a hundred percent on mine." He also said that guys like Sherouse were actually in more danger than guys like him. Sherouse couldn't believe that, but Frontera's logic was that for the same amount of money, a regular dealer had to visit his connection ten times, and he could have turned informant any one of those times. "Me," he told the younger man. "I just have to rob them once." And they couldn't very well go to the cops, could they?

Frontera and John really liked Alex, especially John. Why wouldn't they? He was young, personable, intelligent, spoke Spanish, had connections and, best of all, he was absolutely fearless.

Not long after Alex had sold their product to Olson, he was sitting at the front counter of DTC when he got a call from John. "Meet me in Fort Lauderdale," he said. "And bring a gun."

A few days earlier, a couple of hippyish guys named Eddie and Chip were hanging around some Fort Lauderdale nightclubs and let it be known that were looking to unload 1,500 pounds of weed they had brought up to Miami from their hometown of Islamorada in the Florida Keys. A friend of Frontera's approached them and told them the man they wanted to see was Frontera. With the eagerness of rookies, they asked their new friend to set up a meeting.

The next day, Frontera greeted them and asked for a sample. If the rest of it was as good as the sample, he told them, he'd buy it all. They agreed on a price of $500,000, way higher than market value, and set up a meeting at a cabin the guys had rented in nearby Southwest Ranches.

The setup could hardly be more perfect. It was obvious to Frontera's hardened eye that these two yokels had no idea what they were doing or how far over their heads they were. They might be wannabe drug dealers, but they were anything but badasses. Somehow, they had gotten their hands on almost a ton of premium weed, and Frontera knew it was his for the taking.

He also realized it was the perfect opportunity to bring Alex into the business. Cocaine dealers were tough, well-armed, and ready to protect their product. These two potheads couldn't protect a grizzly bear from a chihuahua.

When Alex arrived in Fort Lauderdale, John told him the plan. Alex was excited and agreed to be part of the team.

They rode out due west just after dark. Frontera and John were in a rented Ryder cube van, while Alex followed discreetly in John's prized possession, his two-week-old Mercedes-Benz 450SEL 6.9. Not to be outdone, Frontera had one just like it at home—both paid cash for what was then just about the most expensive sedan on the market.

Southwest Ranches is still pretty rural even now, but back then it was the backwoods. There were no streetlights on the dirt roads and you were more likely to run into a gator at night than another person—it was, after all, walking distance to the Everglades.

As they approached the cabin, Alex turned the big Benz's head-lights off, followed the truck's taillights, and parked in a spot where the car couldn't be seen by the people inside.

He watched as Eddie welcomed Frontera and John inside the cabin. John even shook his hand on the way in.

Once inside, Eddie and John were surprised to see another person there. It was Chip's girlfriend, Trish. She looked harmless enough. They asked about Chip, and Trish said that he had gone to try to find them all some beer. They believed her, but kept an eye on the doors anyway.

She offered them hits on her joint, and they accepted. John even complimented her on its quality.

Then it was time for the show. Since they were obviously beginners, it would be easy to impress them by acting just like the gangsters did in movies and on TV. Frontera walked over to the dining room table where Trish was sitting and Eddie followed. Frontera set down the briefcase he was carrying and opened it with a flourish. Inside was nothing but cash. It was tied up with rubber bands into bundles, like you see in movies. It was all real, but Frontera had put the big bills, like twenties and fifties, on top and ones and fives underneath. There were also a couple of loose hundreds on top for effect. The purported $500,000 was more like $130,000.

Still, it was enough to impress Eddie, and as he stared at it, Frontera told John to bring the van closer to the door so it would be easier to move the product.

When Alex, not far away, saw John leave the cabin, it was a signal that everything was going according to plan. If he had seen any cops, Alex had been instructed to honk the Mercedes's horn. Since he hadn't, John backed the cube van nearer to the cabin door. That, too, was a sign.

Alex ran past the truck, into the cabin's door and pointed his .45 at Eddie's head. "DEA! Get on the fucking floor now!" he shouted. "Get on the fucking floor! I'm DEA!"

Eddie and Trish were in too much shock to move. Frontera got out of his chair and lay face down on the floor. Once they had regained their senses, Eddie and Trish followed suit.

Alex walked around the cabin, pretending to search it, yelling things like "stay on the fucking floor!" and "I'm serious!" when suddenly two pit bulls came charging out of the cabin's bedroom. Alex was shocked and hesitated. But the dogs couldn't gain a purchase on the hard, slippery pine floor, and their skittering claws gave Alex a chance to react. *Pow. Pow. Pow. Pow. Pow.* He shot both dogs. They went down injured, but still alive.

Frontera sighed and began to get up. Eddie grabbed him and told him not to, clearly thinking Frontera was going to try to save them from the DEA, not realizing that they would never send a single agent into such a dangerous situation.

But Frontera stood up, pulled out his own gun and ordered Eddie and Trish to stay down.

Hearing the sound of gunfire, John came storming into the cabin with his own gun drawn. He surveyed the scene and grinned.

Frontera handed Alex his gun and pulled out some plastic zip ties out of his socks. He used them to bind both the hands and feet of Eddie and Trish.

He then joined John, who was already loading the weed into the truck. Alex stood at the door making sure Eddie and Trish didn't move and that if Chip or some nosy neighbor showed up, they would be taken care of.

When they were done, Frontera jumped into the truck's cab. John leapt into the Mercedes and called for Alex to join him. Once he was inside, they sped out of Southwest Ranches.

Back in Fort Lauderdale, they unloaded the truck at a warehouse they had rented and headed to their usual hangout, O'Hara's Jazz Café (which has since been torn down).

While there, they reveled in their adventures over beers, laughing at Alex shooting the dogs, and how Eddie had pissed himself once the bullets started flying. Most people would be in shock after that kind of ordeal. But not Alex; he thought it was hilarious. And he frequently fell apart laughing while reenacting it.

The next day, Frontera and John treated Alex to a fancy lunch at the Plaza Venetia in Miami. As they were dining on stone crabs, Frontera's beeper went off. He had been expecting a call from

Boston—the guy who he was selling the weed to—but the number was local, it had a 305 area code. Still, he had to call it.

When he came back from the pay phone, he was laughing so hard that he was almost crying. He told the guys that the call had come from none other than Trish. Apparently, Chip had been in the cabin's bedroom the whole time and had sicced the dogs on Alex when everything went down. And, when Alex shot at the dogs, one of the ricochets from the hard floor hit Chip, taking off one of his toes. Now Trish wanted to know what they were going to do about it.

They didn't stop laughing until Frontera's beeper went off again. It was the call from Boston and the buyer wanted the weed as soon as possible.

Alex would make about $35,000 on the deal. Not bad for someone whose legitimate job paid less than $10,000 a year.

But it was more than just money. Alex had found a real reason to get up in the morning. He found a way to use his talents and skills. He was a natural. It was just like wrestling, except it made him rich.

"I didn't just wake up one morning and decide I wanted to deal drugs," Alex later said. But, like cocaine itself, once he started, he found it hard to stop.

CHAPTER 7

Back to School

Coke and weed weren't the only drugs flowing through South Florida at the time. Quaaludes were a brand name for a popular sleeping pill that had been made illegal in the early 1970s after people started abusing them. Taking Quaaludes not only relaxes users and gives them a feeling of comfort, but the pills are also reputed to bring on sexual feelings and to lower inhibitions.

Nicknamed "disco biscuits," Quaaludes were very popular with the rich and famous—both David Bowie and Frank Zappa mentioned them in songs, and Keith Richards was arrested for possessing them. That certainly increased their desirability to the wannabe jet-setters of South Florida at the time.

And Alex eventually had no problem selling every single one he could get his hands on. He'd been participating in rips with John and Frontera for a couple of years, and had developed some strong connections for unloading coke, but Quaaludes were a bit tougher—at least at first.

So, when he had 26,000 of them on his hands for the first time after a rip, he let it be known among the drug cognoscenti of South Florida that he was looking to sell.

After a couple of days, a guy he'd heard of, but didn't really know, got in touch with him. He wanted the pills. Fine, Alex told him, and they set up an exchange in the parking lot of Lester's Diner, a popular comfort food restaurant near the Fort Lauderdale airport.

The buyer showed up a few minutes after Alex arrived. They made the deal, and just as Alex was about to drive off, his car was surrounded by undercover police vehicles. DEA officers came pouring out of them, and even more from Lester's front door.

Alex was armed, but there was no way he could shoot his way out of this situation. They'd pinned him. He was going to jail.

Before that, though, Alex was enjoying the life of a small-time dealer. He'd quit DTC, upgraded his car, upgraded his wardrobe, and upgraded his girlfriend.

He was also getting very close with Scott Sherouse. About a year before Alex hooked up with John and Frontera, Sherouse sold coke for the first time. It all happened because some guy outside of St. Louis had mistakenly heard he was a coke dealer and wanted some and further enticed him by saying that he'd pay top dollar.

Eager to move up a level, Sherouse scrambled into action. Unfortunately for him, Olson was out of town and not reachable before the customer's deadline. So, Sherouse had to buy his cocaine off the street like anyone else. Despite shaking every tree he could find, he was only offered some really low-quality stuff, well below his expectations for purity. But he figured it was better than nothing, so he bought it, and hoped his St. Louis guy either wouldn't check it or just didn't know any better.

Afraid he was being set up for a rip or an arrest, Sherouse met the guy in a hotel and made the exchange. It all happened so fast that the buyer never checked the stuff. Sherouse could have sold him baby powder for all he knew.

Other than Olson not being around, it went off without a hitch. Sherouse had expected to make $1,500, but actually walked off with $5,500—about half a year's pay at the AUTEC shop.

He, too, had found his calling.

That kind of lifestyle didn't tend to lead to long-term romantic relationships—Doddridge was out of the picture by then—but Sherouse thought he could buck the trend. He got married a few days after Christmas 1978. Alex served as his best man. The guys had partied a bit too hard the night before, though, and the happy couple got off to a rocky start.

Alex had enjoyed the ripping and dealing lifestyle for a couple of years until his arrest. Times were different back then, before the War of Drugs escalated in earnest in the Reagan years. Alex was sentenced to what dealers in those days called a "zip-six," which meant that the judge gave him anywhere from no time behind bars to six years, it was up to the prison system to decide how long he stayed incarcerated, if he was going to be at all.

Alex was taken to the Federal Prison Camp, Eglin, which was part of the Air Force base at Eglin on the Florida panhandle not far from Pensacola. It was a minimum security facility and it became nationally recognized as a lenient, even comfortable, place after several of the Watergate conspirators were sent there. *Forbes* magazine reported that it was so cushy that inmates referred to it as "Club Fed"—a play on Club Med, which was a popular all-in-one travel package company. Always controversial after that, it was closed in 2006, and the land and buildings returned to the Air Force.

These days, the federal prison system does its best to separate veteran criminals from first-timers, but it certainly didn't back then. Sending Alex to Eglin was like giving him a full-ride scholarship to a college at which he majored in drug trafficking and minored in money laundering. The old guys, the big players, not only taught him everything they knew about their trades, they also gave him the names and numbers connections on the outside who could make him richer and work with far less risk than the setup he had with John and Frontera.

It didn't all happen right away. Club Fed might have been cushy by federal prison standards, but it was still a federal prison. A couple of tough guys saw this young first-timer show up and thought it might be a good idea to test his mettle. The fights Alex got into at Eglin ended predictably and quickly.

That caught the attention of the guys who mattered. And when Club Fed held its annual "Mini-Olympics" that summer, Alex won all eight events. They weren't even close.

One of his first visitors at Eglin was Jeff Cutler, who was there on official business for another inmate. He had heard Alex was being held there "which was not a complete surprise," and thought his old teammate might appreciate his stopping by. "We had some nice conversations. We caught up on old times and I remember him saying, 'I may not be here that much longer.' We left it at that," Cutler later recalled. "I didn't know if that meant he was going back into the drug business, being in trouble again, or just leaving. But he made it sound like he was moving."

Alex was released after just two years, and hooked up with Sherouse and his other pals again. Although he still worked for John and Frontera from time to time, Alex had learned from the old hands at Eglin that there were easier and safer ways to make money. The older guys in prison who took the time to mentor Alex gave him a huge number of contacts. "Alex knew more people than probably were in the Miami phone directory," said Louis Feher, Frontera's cousin. "He knew everybody, where to go see people that knew other top people that were down in South America."

At the top of his list of potential employers was Ollie Carly "O. C." Davis, one of the biggest drug smugglers in Florida.

Davis was more than happy to host Alex for an interview, as he had come highly recommended by his mutual friends at Eglin. Davis had built his business and became remarkably wealthy by smuggling weed from Jamaica to the Bahamas and then into Florida.

But he was not immune to the siren song of cocaine, and started moving it—and receiving its immense profits—in great quantities.

Traditionally, getting drugs to the United States has not been a big problem, but actually getting them in always has been. Davis, like many others of the era, employed a method known as the airdrop.

Like other countries, the United States' territorial waters extend twelve miles from the shoreline at low tide. Before the UN Convention on the Law of the Sea came into force in 1994 (the United States has not ratified the law, but honors it nonetheless) drug trafficking in international waters was the responsibility of the nation in which the trafficker's vessel was registered.

Back then, the Bahamian authorities didn't have the resources or the will to take down traffickers, and—if they were more than twelve miles from Florida—American law enforcement could merely watch them operate. Or if a trafficker feared that he might be one of the rare guys that the Bahamian authorities did decide to prosecute—maybe he failed to bribe the right guy—he could always register the vessel to some far-off country for a few bucks knowing they wouldn't lift a finger. It's no coincidence that more than 40 percent of the world's shipping, by weight, is registered to Liberia, Panama, or the Marshall Islands.

So, ships from the Bahamas had traditionally gotten as close as they could to the territorial limit, unloaded their cargo to smaller boats posing as anglers or pleasure boaters and let them take the risk of getting the drugs to Florida. With all the boat traffic in the area, it was nearly impossible for the DEA to know which ones were carrying drugs, especially when they had been equipped with purpose-built hidden compartments.

But ships are big and easy to track, and if the Americans are tipped off that one was making a drop-off, they could scoop up many of the smaller craft, leading to significant losses for the traffickers and the potential for arrested boat captains and crew to cooperate with law enforcement to save themselves. It eventually became so commonplace for law enforcement officers to stop pleasure craft, have the guys aboard tell them they were just fishing, search them and then find drugs, that the cops started calling bales of marijuana or cocaine "square grouper."

Since cocaine was so much less bulky than marijuana, traffickers could be a lot stealthier. A single-engine private plane could carry millions of dollars' worth of coke and a twin-engine even more, especially after the passenger seats were removed. They can, and do, fly under traditional radar and can be nearly impossible to detect.

The airdrop requires a pilot to be precise, and to be a bit reckless. When they arrive at the drop spot, it's imperative to have the plane flying as low and as slow as possible to prevent the bales of cocaine from being damaged on impact with the water or becoming lost.

It can be quite the sight. David Lemieux, who would later become Alex's right-hand man, recalls watching as one plane came in, perilously close to the water's surface, and opened its flaps and even lowered its landing gear to increase wind resistance and reduce speed. A first-timer who was with him was sure the crazy pilot was trying to land on the Atlantic Ocean.

No matter how slow they go and how close to the water the planes are, the bales of cocaine make a huge splash—with the spray of water frequently reaching higher than the plane itself—as they are kicked out the door. That makes it easier for the boat captains to find them.

And there's no shortage of captains. A single boatload could be worth millions (Alex and Davis had gotten their drops up to about $24 million, usually divided by four boats), and the simple act of picking up a few bales, getting them the last few miles into Florida, and dropping them off would pay the boat captains more in a day than most jobs did in a couple of years.

And Alex was very good at what he did. He didn't go out in the boats—that was for Lemieux and the rest of the team Alex had put together from trusted friends. Instead, it was his job to coordinate the whole thing from Florida, making calls from parking lot pay phones ranging from Homestead to Boca Raton. Davis's men would tell him where the drop would be, Alex would communicate that to his people, and then tell them where to go. Finally, when they came back, he told them where to bring the product so he could take it from there and get it to his contacts. Although he was never in the water, he got the biggest cut.

That's how drug trafficking worked back them. Alex and his people were movers, not dealers. It wasn't a day-to-day thing, like the guys who stand on corners slinging crack. No, these guys would make a big score and then just hang out until the next opportunity arose or they needed money again.

Once Alex and his friends hooked up with Davis, they weren't small-timers anymore. They were young men with plenty of money and time on their hands. And they did what you'd expect.

They all collected toys, especially cars and boats. After he started working with John and Frontera, Alex had acquired his own Mercedes-Benz 450SEL 6.9 just to keep up, an even more eye-catching Corvette ZR-1 and a 1956 Ford Thunderbird, just like the one he had always admired from the movie *American Graffiti*. He had boats, personal watercraft, anything someone like him could want. Not much later, he bought a Harley-Davidson, which became his preferred mode of transportation.

And they played with those toys all the time. Alex, Sherouse, and their other friends would spend their days on the ocean, fishing or catching conch and then finding a nice beach to grill them on.

After that, it was drinks at a bar such as the Compleat Angler or a night at a gentlemen's club like the Trap Lounge stuffing cash down strippers' underwear.

There were always women around these guys. Just as South Florida had attracted legions of drug dealers, it had also attracted swarms of women attracted to the easy life of money and spare time.

And they loved Alex because he was still Alex. Bold and personable, dressed impeccably, the big man was always surrounded by women. He didn't have to work hard at it, but he did anyway, just because he was Alex. Sherouse recalls an evening at a strip club when Alex stood up and meticulously started covering his table with cash and a few lines of blow. It was an unmistakable message and it looked like feeding time at the zoo. Women got up from the men they were sitting with and rushed to be at Alex's side.

But those women, according to one of Alex's friends and business associates at the time, might not have known exactly what they were in for. "He was very rude and crude, very primitive with women," said Feher. "He used to beat women, sexually, all kinds of things. He'd go crazy. He had no respect for nothing or nobody."

The lifestyle was seductive and addictive. Lemieux later recalled that it didn't feel like they were even breaking laws anymore, that it was just "the Miami lifestyle." Trafficking had become normal for them and everybody they knew.

Alex needed manpower for his operation, and he recruited old friends that he'd wrestled with or against in high school and college. There was something about the guys he had practiced or hit the mat with that he felt he could trust. He had plenty of eager candidates, but the easy money pitch didn't work on everyone. "Alex said, 'We drove to Michigan and we ripped this guy off,'" recalled Andrew DeWitt years later. "I don't want anything to do with this. You could go to jail for this."

But those he did manage to recruit had more money than they knew what to do with and more time to play than they ever imagined, because they'd only ever work for a couple of days every two or three months. At any time of the day or night, if they weren't on the water or a beach or a strip joint, they were in the finest restaurants or the golf course. Sleep was an afterthought.

But while Alex was living the high life of a trafficker, he still had his old job with John and Frontera as a rip-off artist. They called him about a boat, the Dirty Dancing, which was moored behind the Castaways resort hotel up at Sunny Isles Beach, just north of Miami Beach.

When he arrived, Alex was impressed. After all, it takes a lot of money to afford a fifty-six-footer. They were surprised to find that there was nearly a half ton of cocaine on board. It was worth millions, and Alex and his team took every single speck.

But it would be his last rip. Despite what Frontera had told Sherouse, Alex knew it was just too dangerous. Pulling a gun, shouting that you're DEA—that's a pretty good way to get shot. And when you leave with their drugs and money and nobody gets arrested, the dealers know exactly what had really happened. Word gets around, faces start matching verbal descriptions, maybe you run into the wrong guy at a bar. There couldn't have been too many people around who looked that much like Alex. It would only be a matter of time before he made enough powerful enemies; guys who were getting tired of losing their shipments and risking their own lives to pay back the Colombians.

Alex retired from the rip-off game because the money from coordinating drops was easier to get and the job was safer. All he had to do was find a pay phone, call the right people, sit back and make big money. It was as close as he could get to having a desk job in the cocaine trafficking industry.

CHAPTER 8

Casualties of War

Just like Alex, Kevin came back to South Florida a changed man. Not only had he graduated from West Point, he had done so with flying colors, having received good marks, and, far more important, letters of recommendation from his instructors. Upon completion of his studies, he was a brand new second lieutenant in the US Army. He had the start of the summer of 1980 off to await assignment.

West Point had changed more than just his status. It changed him fundamentally. Although he still preferred his own company, Kevin was no longer shy and introverted. He stood his ground, and took better than he gave in social situations, just as he always had on the mat.

But his father hadn't changed at all. It was early in the evening, just after Kevin had returned to Pinecrest and Myron was already getting hammered, as he did every night. Kevin knew it wouldn't be long before he started in on him with his incessant criticism.

Kevin hated living with Myron, but he was just in Miami for a short stay until his orders came through, so it was logical (and economical) for him to take up residence in his old room at his parents' house. Besides, he had to save money if he was going to provide for Betty and Danny the way he wanted to.

He'd only been under his father's roof for a few hours, and already he was regretting his decision. Kevin didn't want to sit around and watch his dad devolve into a slurring, stumbling bully, so he decided to step out for a while, and maybe come back and have some quiet time with his mom after his dad had passed out like he did every night.

Despite his father's raging alcoholism, Kevin had actually had acquired a taste for a beer himself. He had his first beer at a party at the Naval Academy. He liked it so much, he got staggeringly drunk and puked in a decorative flower planter.

One of the things he had learned pretty quickly at West Point is that if you wanted to succeed as an officer in the US Army, drinking was an absolute requirement. After his first time, Kevin became a more responsible drinker. He wasn't an inveterate drunk like his old man, but he did enjoy a beer or two every now and then, just found it to be relaxing, so he figured he'd head out to a bar and practice being an Army officer.

The obvious place for him to go that night would have been Keg South—a woody sports bar where all the old wrestlers and their coaches went. He'd be known there, he'd have friends there. Everyone would want to shake his hand and pat him on the back and ask his all about what it was like at West Point and what he thought the army had in store for him.

But no matter how positive and genuine their feelings would be, Kevin just didn't want that kind of attention right then. He needed some alone time, some time to himself to recharge his batteries. He needed to be away from home, from Myron, from everyone and everything. Just him, his thoughts, and a cold beer or two.

So instead of heading south, he drove north. About the same distance from his house as Keg South, but in the complete opposite direction, he pulled into the parking lot at a bar called the Crown Lounge. He'd never been there before in his life, didn't even know it even existed, but it seemed all right from the outside. It was quiet and dark and had some nice-looking cars parked out front.

As he got out of his car, Kevin realized how ridiculous he must have looked to the people inside the bar, caught up as they no doubt would be in the new Miami. Kevin had received his orders. He was headed to the 24th Infantry Division in October and his appearance did nothing but reflect that. "I was probably the only man in the entire region with short hair," he later said—and his was Army-regulation shaved-to-the-skin short. He had combined that look with a white T-shirt with the word "Airborne" and a pair of wings across the front. Kevin was proud to have been through airborne training and jump school, and didn't even spare a thought as to what people would think about his shirt. And to cap it all off, he was wearing jeans that had to be at least four years out of date in trendy Miami. Jeans were not allowed at West Point, so the ones Kevin wore in high school were still waiting for him in his dresser when he came home.

At the time, serving in the military was seen as social suicide over much of America, and intensely so in more progressive areas, like what Miami had become in his absence. As Jimmy Carter's presidency was sputtering to a close, the American military did not hold the country's attention and admiration the way it once had. The debacle in Vietnam was still a recent and very painful memory; the Russians had invaded Afghanistan and all we did about it was boycott the Olympic games in Moscow; and fifty-two Americans were still being held hostage in Iran after the crash of the rescue helicopter, resulting in eight dead men and the worldwide media running a photo of some Iranian jerk holding a piece of landing gear over his head in some bizarre form of triumph.

In slick, cocaine-cool Miami at the time, Kevin stuck out far worse than even the sorest thumb. But he didn't really care all that much. He came for some alone time and a cold beer or two. He realized that the more he looked like the man who he had really become at West Point, the less likely it would be that anyone would bother him.

As he walked in the bar, Kevin's quick recon determined that there was a mostly empty seating area to the left, an unoccupied stage in the back and a long bar on the right. There was a loud, gold- and Armani-drenched group of four or five people at the far end of the bar. Exactly the kind of people he wanted to avoid.

He sat down at the bar as far away from them as possible, and ordered a Bud Light. Convinced that he would finally have a few minutes' peace, Kevin took a sip and started to try to unwind, and put Myron out of his mind.

He could hear the group at the end of the bar talking. They turned out to be exactly what he thought they'd be: a bunch of people celebrating with the conscious self-importance of newly acquired wealth. The group was made up of men and women, and they were all surrounding the one big guy who was obviously the most important of the group. He was their leader, the one with charisma, and the rest of them were just his entourage. They were so annoying with their know-nothing talk, their backwards pride in their illegal, anything-but-moral lifestyle, that it made Kevin physically sick. He told me that he even mumbled, "Oh, God" to himself under his breath.

Kevin realized he had to get out of there. He decided to finish his beer and then head out to Keg South, where he was beginning to think he should have gone in the first place.

And then he heard it: "Hey, Ped!"

Kevin knew who it was, but at the same time, he told me, he couldn't believe it. He certainly didn't want to. Nobody else ever called him Ped. And Alex never called him anything but Ped. Never Kevin or Kev or Pedersen or anything else, just Ped.

Then he called again, "Hey, Ped!"

Realizing that his voice was coming from the group of criminal types, Kevin thought just one word to himself: *Shit*.

It was Alex, all right. Of course, it had to be. Of the thousands of bars in Miami he could have chosen that night, Kevin happened to walk into this one while his old wrestling buddy was holding court with his cocaine-chic associates.

Kevin walked over; he was still automatically very obedient in the days right after leaving West Point, though his radar was up, scoping the situation for any signs of trouble. He took his beer with him—hell, a second lieutenant made just $650 a month back then, and he intended to get every penny's worth.

Alex was still huge, actually bigger than Kevin remembered. Wearing a trendy black-on-black outfit and lots of gold jewelry, he looked very much like the drug dealer other friends had hinted to Kevin that he had become.

And as much as it was clear who Kevin was by what he looked like, it was even more obvious what Alex was. Kevin later told me that he couldn't hold on to hope or denial any longer. Alex was clearly a drug dealer, and, by the looks of him, a very successful one.

When Kevin approached him with an outstretched hand, he did that thing Kevin said that the Latino men he knew often did—he pushed his outstretched hand away and engulfed him in a big, affectionate bear hug. Kevin recalled distinctly feeling like a fool as Alex's massive arms were around him as his own hanged limply in front of him.

As much as they had been through together and as close as they had once been, Kevin just couldn't return his hug. Simply put, Alex was a drug dealer, and that represented at this moment a threat to everything Kevin held dear, his own happiness and sense of right and wrong.

Alex immediately introduced Kevin to his coterie of friends, but he later told me he was forgetting their names even as he was hearing them. Alex offered to buy him a beer, even though Kevin noticed Alex and his group were drinking something quite a bit more expensive.

After a moment or so, Alex's entourage, slow-witted as they might have been, took the hint and left the two old pals alone to talk. But they didn't have much to say to each other. Alex asked Kevin how West Point was, but there was no way he could explain such a profound experience over a few minutes in a bar. Instead, Kevin just told him that it was quite a challenge, but it had made him into a second lieutenant in the United States Army and that he was proud of that.

Kevin asked Alex about what was going on with his life. He wouldn't go into any details, but the big man said that he was doing great and that his life was wonderful.

"Really?" Kevin asked him. He told him that he heard his dad had died and that he'd quit college.

Alex made it clear that he didn't want to talk about his father or what he was doing with his life. Instead, he deflected Kevin's question, taking the cigar out of his mouth, and staring at, or rather into, the big wooden bar. After a slow sigh, Alex said: "Well, you and Cut One did things your way..."

Cut One was Jeff Cutler. Alex had made nicknames for everyone on the wrestling team and thought it would be fun to call Cutler "Cut One"—it was a fart joke, like he had just "cut one." Cutler was a year ahead of Kevin and Alex in high school, and a real "by the books" kind of guy who had never really gotten along with free-wheeling, rule-bending Alex.

"You went to West Point and now he's in law school." He sighed again, momentously. "I'm doing things my own way ... and I will be OK."

As if to put an exclamation point on his statement, Alex stood up, smiled at Kevin and put out his big old stogie on his own forehead.

Kevin knew he had to get out of there. He hurriedly said good-bye and left. As he was going, Kevin later told me that he could hear Alex's entourage re-collect around their leader, laughing and asking who the guy with the buzz cut was.

Kevin was stunned. His old friend, the guy he looked up to most, had become in his eyes, a "small man." He was greatly disappointed at the path Alex had taken, breaking the law to make himself rich when there were so many important things in the world that needed taking care of.

Driving home, Kevin came to a realization that would be one of the most important guiding forces for the rest of his life. Although he had been trained to fight the Russians at West Point, and everybody was talking about the threat from Iran in those days, he believed he knew who America's real enemies were—the drug smugglers, importers, and dealers—the people who were poisoning its people, ruining its economy and shooting it out on its streets. The wave of drug traffickers wasn't a threat anymore; they had already invaded and were winning the war on our own streets.

He didn't completely articulate it at the time, but Kevin told me he already knew deep inside of himself that he had chosen to be on one side of the war, and that his old friend, protector, and mentor had abandoned him and chosen to be on the other side.

And, although Kevin didn't want it to be true, he firmly believed that Alex was letting himself be drawn into a situation against opponents he didn't have a chance to beat. Kevin was sure that no matter how hard he tried, Alex would end up on the wrong end of a gun, if not one of the heavily armed Colombian drug gangs, then one of the US government's anti-drug law enforcement squads.

*   *   *

Kevin was too busy to worry about Alex, though. He had a fiancée and a new son to get to know and plans for their future together to make. Kevin and Betty were married in a small, but joyous ceremony on October 25, 1980, just a few days before his orders indicated he had to ship out to Fort Stewart in Georgia.

It seemed to everyone, not the least of all Kevin, that he had everything he ever wanted. But it wasn't going to last.

Things went well for Kevin in Georgia, and he excelled at leadership. There was one incident involving enlisted men that gave him pause, though. After a grueling day in the Georgia heat, some of the enlisted men he commanded set up a bivouac and found themselves one cot short. Two privates fought over the last one, and one of the men pulled a knife and killed the other.

Kevin was called in, assessed the situation, got everything under control, and followed the rulebook to the letter. He even called the dead man's wife to let her know.

Still thinking about how the influx of drug money had changed South Florida, the stabbing put things into perspective for Kevin— if an ordinary guy would kill another man for a decent night's sleep, what would he do for the millions of dollars coming in from the Atlantic Ocean?

America was changing. The Iran hostage crisis ended the day after hardline Republican president Ronald Reagan was inaugurated in January 1981, but the lessons from the US military's impotence in that era weighed heavily on its commanders. They realized that it had become critical for the US Army to develop a quick-strike capability that could act anywhere in the world, rapidly, without warning and with real power.

The 24th, along with the 82nd Airborne and 101st Airborne were selected to be part of the new rapid deployment force. That led to Kevin being deployed quickly, and without notice, to spots all over the world.

His own unit was the 52nd Air Defense Artillery Regiment—armed with Vulcan Gatling gun systems and FIM-43 Redeye surface-to-air missiles that specialized in taking out low-flying airplanes and helicopters—was then sent to Fort Bliss, near El Paso, Texas. He was promoted to executive officer, battery commander, and platoon leader. Kevin was living the life he had set out to all those years ago when he put up his West Point poster in his bedroom. "I loved leading troops," he would later say. "I loved the camaraderie; I loved being in charge." He proudly pointed out that his platoon was rated the No. 1 platoon in the all of the anti-aircraft units in the entire army.

Betty and Danny Pedersen came along. Betty was still receiving her payments from Bell South and quickly found connections for coke among the military wives and various hangers-on in nearby El Paso. Her respiratory condition worsened, accelerated by her drug use, and she found herself checking into the base medical facility frequently for overnight stays.

After one of those episodes, Kevin was asked to report to his superior officer. Because of his wife's health, the army would no longer allow him to be deployed overseas. He was, they told him, needed at home, with his family. Danny could not be left alone in the country with his mother in the hospital and his father in the Middle East.

Kevin knew it was useless to try to argue.

The army offered him an administrative job, in which he could be close to Betty and Danny and able to react quickly if something went wrong.

Kevin politely declined. "If I couldn't be a combat arms officer, and lead troops, I didn't see the need to be in the army," he said.

He really didn't have any other training or experience, so he approached his father-in-law, who owned three Goodyear Tire and Service Center outlets in suburban South Florida. He agreed to let Kevin work at one in Homestead, not far from the base where Myron had been stationed in his final years with the Air Force.

To his surprise, Kevin didn't mind operating a civilian business. Jim, his father-in-law, ran the front of the business, dealing with customers, while Kevin took care of the back. The two got along very well. "He was pretty grateful to have me back in his daughter's life, instead of that other guy and to know that his grandson had a real dad," Kevin told me

But moving Betty back into South Florida, and this time with more money, put her in a cocaine candy store. She quickly began to show the outward signs of cocaine dependence. She was pale and unhealthy looking, suffered from the sniffles constantly and had many nosebleeds and had mood swings that went from manic happiness to deeply bitter anger in an instant. She couldn't make good decisions; she was failing as a mother.

Kevin's friends and family, especially his brother, Mike, saw what was going on, recognized it and tried to get Kevin to do something about it. But he didn't, he couldn't. Betty was the only woman he ever dated, let alone loved, so leaving her wasn't an option.

But then it got to him and he could take it no longer. He knew that Betty had become dependent on cocaine again and that she was powerless to stop, and he was unable to help her. A future with him and Betty together looked a lot bleaker for both of them, and Danny, than it did with them apart. Kevin filed for divorce.

He wasn't just leaving Betty, but he had to believe she'd get custody of Danny, too, although he would, of course, fight. She'd get the house. And he couldn't very well go on working for her father, Jim, if he wasn't his son-in-law anymore. "I knew I was going to get fired. You don't divorce the owner's daughter and think they're going to keep you on the job," he said. "So, I had a pretty good idea I was going to lose my position. Even though we had built the business up and her father was my best friend."

Kevin felt like an abject failure. "To fail at a marriage is a devastating thing," he would later say. "Because I thought that was one of the most important things in life." At thirty-one years old, he moved himself into a lonely little one bedroom apartment in Homestead.

His current living situation ate away at him constantly. He had lost everything. Wrestling was gone. The army was gone, his wife and even his child were gone. He had no hope, no job, no way out.

His friends and family were concerned for him, afraid he might take a drastic step. His brother, Mike, recalled him saying, "life's not worth living" and other alarming phrases.

After his last day at Jim's shop, he made his way home to his little apartment with no idea what he would do the following day or any day after that. Alone, unemployed, weeping, stone-cold sober, he got down on his knees in the middle of his little unit.

Then he pulled out a Colt Commando nine-millimeter revolver—one of his many guns—put a round in the chamber and pressed the end of the barrel against his right temple. *This is the easy way out*, he thought to himself.

CHAPTER 9

Miami Vice

Despite all the time they spent partying, Alex and his boys could usually be found at home on the couch from 10 o'clock until 11 on Friday nights—or least in a bar where they could control what was on the TV. That's because they rarely missed their favorite show—*Miami Vice*.

Debuting five years and two months after the Dadeland Mall shooting, *Miami Vice* was an instant hit nationwide, reaching ninth place in the overall TV ratings, which was an almost impossible feat at the time for a post-prime time show.

Widely praised for its slick integration of popular music and a look inspired by contemporary music videos, the show was considered visually stunning at the time. *People* magazine raved about it, saying it was the "first show to look really new and different since color TV was invented."

A big part of the show's immediate success came from how the two handsome leads—Don Johnson and Philip Michael Thomas, who played Sonny Crockett and Rico Tubbs, undercover detectives posing as big-time traffickers—looked and lived. Much of the show was shot in Miami, and it looked absolutely stunning.

Johnson and Thomas dressed stylishly, in a way unseen by the rest of the country before, but soon copied and made almost universally standard for young American men for years. They wore Armani or Versace suits or sports coats with tailored pants and, instead of collared shirts and ties, they wore designer T-shirts or mock turtlenecks. And much of their wardrobe was made up of tropical-inspired colors such as fuchsia and aqua that men outside of Florida would not have been caught dead in previously. In an interview years later, Johnson said that he saw a picture of himself from the era in a loose-fitting pastel suit, and thought, *Why was I wearing pajamas?*

Johnson and Thomas wore $600 shoes without socks. Then so did everyone else. They sported five o'clock shadows and dripped with gold. Both looks quickly became popular. So influential were their fashion choices that Ebel actually outbid Rolex to have Johnson's character switch to their expensive watch on the show instead of the Rolex he had been sporting in hopes that it would boost sales.

Crockett and Tubbs drove Ferraris and Porsches, they swanned about in speedboats, dined in the finest restaurants, danced in the most exclusive nightclubs, and seemed to have unlimited time, women, and cash on their hands.

The tacit message was that the cops on *Miami Vice* were so incredibly cool because they looked and acted a lot like the way drug traffickers do in Miami. They were the real cool guys.

Miami, the sleepy southern town Johnny Carson used to mock on the *Tonight Show* for being full of white-belted retirees had suddenly become the coolest, most happening city in North America. As *Miami Vice* co-creator Anthony Yerkovich explained to *Time* magazine:

Even when I was on Hill Street Blues, I was collecting information on Miami, I thought of it as a sort of a modern-day
American Casablanca. It seemed to be an interesting socio-
economic tide pool: the incredible number of refugees from
Central America and Cuba, the already extensive Cuban-
American community, and on top of all that the drug trade.
There is a fascinating amount of service industries that revolve
around the drug trade—money laundering, bail bondsmen,
attorneys who service drug smugglers. Miami has become a
sort of Barbary Coast of free enterprise gone berserk.

And the real dealers and traffickers in Miami loved it. Alex tried
not to miss a single episode. His favorite parts, I would learn, were
those times when art imitated life, which often imitated it back.

He and his friends would take names from the show to use in
their everyday lives. When something went wrong, they would
always blame Calderone, the unseen mastermind who so bedeviled
the show's protagonists.

As had happened several times before, Alex was both shocked and
delighted by something very familiar he saw on the evening of March
27, 1987. In an episode titled "Knock, Knock . . . Who's There?" the
main characters—Crockett and Tubbs—are investigating a trafficker
when two DEA agents storm the nightclub, and demand everyone
hit the ground. They zip-tied everyone, even Crockett and Tubbs,
and made off with everyone's drugs and cash. When Crockett realizes
the men never showed them any badges, it dawns on him that they
weren't DEA agents after all; they were a couple of rip artists.

Alex hooted in laughter and asked the collected crowd of his
entourage, "Who told the *Miami Vice* writers?" about what he had
done for years with John and Frontera.

* * *

You might think that the violence in Miami would scare people off, but just about the time that the cocaine wars began, Miami's population exploded.

Part of that growth was due to a historic event that was later called the Mariel Boatlift. It started with a small number of activists desperate to leave Cuba and ended up changing the face of South Florida.

In early 1980, a few Cubans started protesting Castro's government and the fact that it was illegal to move out of the country by entering the grounds of foreign embassies. Since embassies are technically the territory of the country whose flag flies there, the Cuban officials could not force them to leave although they did kill two men attempting to enter the Argentine embassy and fired on crowds who had crashed a bus into the gate of the Venezuelan embassy to gain access to its grounds.

Before long, the number of Cubans who sought refuge at the Peruvian embassy alone grew to 10,800 people living in little more than squalid standing room.

Under pressure, an embarrassed Castro decided to act. In a move he referred to as "magnanimous" on his part, he announced that any Cuban who wanted to leave the country could, provided they not leave by any state-owned airline or water vessel. But because it was a communist country that essentially denounced the concept of private property, all aircraft and virtually every seagoing vessel were owned by the state. It was a Catch-22.

Castro also announced that anyone who departed through the port of the city of Mariel would be allowed to leave without any interference. But he announced that fact only to the foreign press; not to anyone in Cuba, other than his inner circle.

Many crafty Cubans, however, saw through his doublespeak and political tricks. Cuban-Americans living in Florida broadcast frequent and unjammable radio messages informing Cubans about the

Mariel amnesty zone announcement. And the Cubans themselves built their own watercraft of varying degrees of seaworthiness. To many of them, it was better to risk death in some rickety raft on the high seas than to stay in Cuba.

US president Jimmy Carter, already very unpopular, agreed to accept 3,500 of the refugees, announcing a plan to vet them through Costa Rica first.

That never happened. Instead, an official count of 124,779 Cubans arrived directly on Florida's many beaches. The standing US policy was to offer refugee status to any Cuban who was able to reach the United States, so the National Guard, Red Cross, Roman Catholic Church, and other organizations were employed to process them and find places for them all, using football stadiums and even decommissioned military bases for the task.

It was a controversial event. The left criticized Carter for treating Cubans, mostly white and Christian, with preferential treatment, when there were much needier people in the world. The right criticized him for being unable to control the size of the influx and the lack of national security in the area. And both sides just about lost their cool when American reporters from PBS found out that after the exodus started, the Castro regime began to bus maximum security prisoners and mental hospital patients to Mariel and even provided them with seaworthy boats.

There was little either side could do about it, though. There were almost 125,000 Cubans in South Florida who were well on their way to becoming Cuban Americans. Miami, a city in which Cubans had been a small minority just a few years earlier, would soon have a Cuban American plurality.

It's true that some of the Marielitos were murderers and gangsters, as many feared, but the overwhelming majority was not. Among the refugees were Bárbaro Garbey, a future major league baseball player and coach, and Mirta Ojito, who later became a much-celebrated

Pulitzer Prize winner, and many others became notable people, although most were just rank-and-file Miamians after a while.

It wasn't just the refugees who came to Miami at the time. People such as Frontera came for the easy money available in trafficking. But even more came just because the wave of cocaine that swept over Miami brought with it a tsunami of money and the cool life-style they saw on *Miami Vice*. Why be a waiter in Minneapolis, when, in Miami, the weather is beautiful and the traffickers tip more than your daily salary for every meal? Why be a stripper in St. Louis when the guys in Miami spent thousands at the club every night? Why sell Fords in Denver when you can sell Ferraris on South Beach? Miami was glamorous, the place to be. Anyone could get rich there, even if they weren't breaking the law.

Alex and Sherouse were very popular, and were invited out frequently. They found themselves at the house of a mutual friend in Coconut Grove, and Alex saw what he called the most beautiful girl he had ever seen by the host's pool. It was Linda Lieberher, who was a couple of grades ahead of him at Palmetto.

They hit it off and before long he had a son (also named Daniel, and called Danny, just like Kevin's). The happy couple was soon married on a luxurious yacht Alex had rented. But, like Sherouse's own wife, Linda would be quickly frustrated with her new husband. The morning after their wedding, Alex told her had to go do a job. Unable to go on the honeymoon to Hawaii that he had already paid for, his new wife took her sister instead.

Alex knew that if he wanted to get super-rich, he had to traffic, so he dedicated himself to it.

But Sherouse did not share his limitless ambition, and was later scared out of the game.

One afternoon, they were hanging out at Alex's place watching *Scarface*—the 1983 film about a Cuban immigrant from the Mariel Boatlift who made millions from coke in Miami. It's a film that is greatly beloved by traffickers even today. When the movie came to the infamous scene in which a rival dealer is tied to a motel room shower nozzle and shredded with chainsaws, Alex freaked out, pointed at the TV and started laughing uncontrollably. It was, as he pointed out to Sherouse, the same hotel where they had staged a rip just weeks earlier.

It really was. Alex and Sherouse had threatened some dealers and took their drugs at 728 Ocean Drive, just two rooms down from the one director Brian De Palma had used for one of the most memorably violent scenes in movie history.

Alex thought it was hilarious. He might even have been a bit proud to be associated with *Scarface*. It's one thing to be in a popular, big-budget Hollywood movie, but it's another thing entirely to be portrayed in such a film.

The scene and how close it was to their adventures in trafficking also hit Sherouse close to home, but he didn't find it at all funny. Perhaps it was the shock and horror of seeing someone torn to pieces a few feet from where he had risked his own life just weeks before, but he decided to get out of the drug business. The violence, he could see, was too much for him and was only going to get worse. Sherouse did not share Alex's fearless abandon.

But it's not that easy to retire from the trafficking business. Sherouse could probably go back to a nine-to-five job repairing boats for $10,000 a year or so, but it would be an abrupt lifestyle change, a shock even, for someone who had gotten used to working one or two days a month and spending the rest fishing and partying, sometimes spending $10,000 in a single night.

The only way he could retire, he realized, would be to make one final huge score, padding his bank account so he could ease into civilian life. He decided that he'd pull his own rip. When Alex and he brought in a huge shipment, Sherouse took 220 kilos from it and left.

He wouldn't have a hard time getting rid of it. The culture of traffickers in South Florida back in the day was very hush-hush. Nobody except the biggest players knew anything more than they had to. They moved the product and that was it. They had no idea who supplied it or who beyond their primary contact was going to get it. That kept anyone who was arrested from sharing too much information with law enforcement.

Alex, as was his nature, found humor in the situation. When a particularly big load would come in he'd say that that it "must be from Pablo"—because everybody knew that only the notorious Colombian drug lord Pablo Escobar had the capability to move the biggest loads of cocaine.

These days, Sherouse says that he didn't intend to cheat Alex. It might sound like a rationalization now, but his plan, he said, was to cut Alex in after the fact.

When Alex finally got him on the phone, he asked his old wrestling buddy where he was and what had happened. He was worried, he said. Sherouse told him that he was fine and that he had taken the 220 kilos so that they could retire together. He had a plan, he assured Alex. With the millions they would soon have, they could get out of South Florida, buy some properties and get rich flipping houses—all legal and, better yet, safe.

Alex was having none of it. He knew that the Colombians either had to be paid or people would start getting killed. He told Sherouse that if they didn't deliver, heads would roll.

Sherouse scoffed. Nobody they knew had ever been killed, he pointed out, and rips happened all the time. And none of the Colombians they worked with seemed all that badass to him, so he held his ground. If Alex wasn't going to join him, he said, he'd keep all 220 kilos for himself.

When he couldn't get Sherouse to change his mind, Alex made the incredibly bold choice of going to his supplier and telling him exactly what had happened.

As violent as the Colombian cartels were, they did not go out of their way to kill people who they knew can help them, and they must have been impressed by how courageous and forthright Alex had been. Besides, he was an incredibly valuable asset. It was decided that Alex would stay alive and employed as long he paid off the 220 kilos Sherouse had stolen through labor. Alex eagerly agreed.

Although Sherouse's theft had cost Alex a lot of time and money in the short term, it also put him on the map as a man of his word and an asset. Here was an American citizen—equally fluent in English and Spanish—who not only was extremely skilled and talented at moving product, but who adhered to a standard of honor at the expense of his own time and money, literally risking his own life to do what was right (among the surreal world of drug traffickers, that is). "I know the clear line between right and wrong. I'm not going to walk into the store and walk out without paying for [anything]," Alex later said. "During my days of criminal activity, I tried to bend everything around—fake IDs, fake name—everything was corruptible with money back then, so my sense of normalcy is very different from normal working people."

If anything, his owning up for his ex-partner's perfidy made Alex something of a star. After the Sherouse incident, everybody in Colombia wanted to work with Alex. One, in particular, made a strong push, and Alex was definitely listening.

Julio César Nasser David, the son of Lebanese immigrants who farmed and sometimes smuggled coffee, was known as "El Turco" (the Turk) or "The Old Man." Through hard work and ruthless violence, he had risen to become the undisputed head of the Cartel de la Costa Atlántica, what North Americans call the North Coast Cartel. It was an enviable title, in no small part because shipping from Colombia's north coast is the easiest way to get cocaine to the United States.

He was a big deal. The DEA credits him with innovating the concept of parking a freighter outside of the United States' territorial waters and offloading onto a flotilla of smaller boats. "Julio was the father of the mother ship," DEA agent Gary Wade told the *New York Times*.

Before him, cocaine went directly to the US via low-flying planes that landed in remote airfields under the cover of darkness. Not only were they increasingly easy to intercept, but their loads were small. Nasser David was largely responsible for turning the trickle of cocaine entering the United States into a torrent by using freighters instead of personal aircraft.

He was so wealthy and employed so many people in money laundering that he actually decided to buy controlling interest a bank in South Florida just to ease the burden of paperwork.

Nasser David bored easily and found that feats of huge volumes or extreme boldness were just about the only way he could stay interested in the business. Félix "La Mica" (the Flirt) Chitiva Carrasquilla—one of Nasser David's top men, and later a close friend and business associate of Alex's—later recalled that he boldly took maybe a hundred tons of Nasser David's weed hundreds of miles up the Mississippi in a barge in broad daylight, and he and his crew were flown back to Colombia in private jets after the drop-off.

Word about Alex made it back to Nasser David in Barranquilla. Intrigued, he sent Chitiva to Miami to propose a working arrangement. It didn't take long for him to find Alex. After they got to know each other and became friends, Chitiva told him that Nasser David would like to meet him in Colombia.

Alex quickly agreed, but told him that a Colombian stamp on an American's passport was a black mark in those days. Any American, especially a South Floridian, who had visited Colombia would be thoroughly searched every time they went to an airport and it would probably be enough to get the cops a warrant to put him under surveillance at home.

Chitiva told him that the cartels were well aware of that, and that steps had been made to prevent Alex from getting into trouble.

The pair took a flight from Miami to Caracas, the capital of Venezuela, which was not a major cocaine transit hub at the time, and then drove along the north coast of South America for almost an entire day until they arrived in Barranquilla. Crossing the border was simple, a few dollars exchanged, a few weapons shown, and there would be no Colombian stamp on any passports.

They pulled up to a Lebanese restaurant named Byblos with about two dozen heavily and obviously armed guys out front. The restaurant was lavish, and the table in the middle was piled high with sumptuous food and expensive wines. There were a couple of belly dancers entertaining, but no customers.

Alex, nervous, sat at the table. Within moments, he was joined by Nasser David.

Alex later told friends in Miami that he was surprised by how cool Nasser David was. After all, he had pictured something different from a cartel kingpin who, he said, "had a name like a Roman Emperor." Instead of being brash and high-handed, he was pleasant, polite and charming—even, on occasion, soft-spoken and self-effacing.

They talked and ate and enjoyed the dancers' performances and really hit it off. Nasser David took him on a tour of his own compound, in which he pointed out the cemetery he had built for people who had crossed him. There were plenty of headstones in it already.

The two men had, Alex learned, very compatible philosophies and opinions when it came to trafficking, among other subjects. Nasser David explained to Alex that he had an English-speaking American citizen in Miami who had been doing work for him, but he was not a professional like he had heard Alex was. They called him "the Zombie" because he would take all of his cash from trafficking, invest it in heroin, and stay high on it until he ran out and had to go back to work only because he needed cash again for more heroin. It was time to replace him, Nasser David said, and Alex was his choice.

Alex returned to South Florida—again via Caracas—recharged and was intensely optimistic about his future in the business.

Nasser David had lots of friends and contacts in the Bahamas, including the chief of police of Bimini (the set of Bahamian islands closest to Florida)—Glen "the Sheriff" Rolle. They had a deal. For $40,000, Rolle would allow Nasser David's planes to use his airport without interference from Bahamian authorities. And, in the unlikely event that one or his men or aircraft ran into trouble with a local cop out to shake things up, Rolle would fix it. Anyone caught would be freed, their aircraft returned and, most of the time at least, their cocaine would be given back. It was easier to do illegal business in Bimini than it was to do legitimate business just about anywhere.

Having Alex in Miami, though, gave the ever-ambitious Nasser David an idea. He owned a 236-foot freighter known as the M/V Nerma for years. It had a Danish crew and was registered in the tiny South Pacific island nation of Vanuatu (a little more than eight thousand miles from Miami).

Nasser David had used the Nerma to smuggle coffee and then later, marijuana into the United States through Bimini for years. Of course, the contraband was always in a hidden compartment surrounded by legitimate cargo, making it harder to find, and the ship was rarely inspected closely because its papers were in order— besides, it would have already dropped off the drugs long before it made it to port. It had been little problem for Nasser David to move 1,200 or even more kilos of weed per trip that way.

Besides, the idea of using a freighter to transport cocaine hadn't occurred to anyone yet, on either side of the law. And when they went looking for traffickers, they were not looking for a bunch of Danes guiding a freighter full of bananas up to Jacksonville.

With someone more competent and reliable than the Zombie on the ground in Miami, what was stopping him from filling its massive hold with cocaine instead? Nothing, he decided, and he told Alex to prepare for a lot of cocaine to come his way. For reference, that much cocaine would be about the size of a small SUV.

In June 1988, Alex would get his first load from the Nerma. According to Lemieux, the Nerma would sail to a predetermined point in the Berry Islands, a chain of mostly uninhabited islands in the northern Bahamas visited mostly by divers and big game sport fishers.

The Nerma itself wouldn't stop. It would slow to about four knots, about the same pace as gentle jog, allowing the smaller boat to cruise alongside it. When they were in position, the Nerma's crane would swing a bundle of cocaine wrapped in a net over the awaiting boat and drop it. The Nerma would then continue to its next legitimate stop, Jacksonville, as though nothing had happened and drop off its bananas.

The boat with the cocaine would then sail through Bahamian waters, where Lemieux, by this time Alex's right-hand man, would divide it into smaller portions to be taken to various locations extending all the way from Palm Beach down to the Keys in hidden compartments of small pleasure craft. When he was finished, he'd report to Alex in Miami, who would coordinate with contacts in Florida. Each landing spot would also have a spotter boat that would warn Alex if there was any law enforcement in the area. If there was, he would direct the boat with cocaine to another location.

Once landed, the cocaine was taken to warehouses or safehouses where it would then be loaded into a fleet of inconspicuous white vans, which would take it to a barn on a farm Alex and Frontera had purchased in Ocala, in the center of the state. There it would be divided, and given to couriers to take it to buyers all over the United States.

After the first shipment by the Nerma was successful, Alex was vaulted into the big leagues. Lemieux, his second-in-command, made so much money that he started a successful horse racing operation from his share of the proceeds. Not bad for being in the water for two days.

Not long after, Jaromir John—Alex's old rip buddy—was released from prison, and dropped by, looking for work. Alex didn't hesitate to put him on the payroll; John knew the trafficking business inside and out. He acted as armed security when Alex needed it and even loaded vans with product.

But his primary task was to facilitate stash houses. He'd scan the local newspaper classified ads for rentals and showed up with a story about how his family needed a place to stay because they were leaving, escaping really, from communist Czechoslovakia and desperately needed a place to stay right away. It was a story that appealed to many Americans—and he paid in cash, often more than what the landlord had asked for—so he never had a problem finding a suitable house.

He'd then use the houses to drop off and distribute the cocaine, usually moving in a few girls he knew from the nightclubs and strip joints to give the whole operation an air of normalcy to neighbors. It was even better if they had children.

While Alex was making big money with Nasser David, he was still working for O. C. Davis, who had opened a business, O. C.'s Marina, in the area. Much to the delight of everyone involved, the producers of Miami Vice would sometimes keep the boats used in the show at his marina.

Lemieux recalls that he was hanging out at the marina when he got a call from someone in one of the boats who was having engine trouble. He went out into the bay to see what was wrong, and was surprised to find that the boater was none other than Don Johnson, the instantly recognizable star of *Miami Vice*. According to Lemieux, Johnson hadn't bothered to check if the boat had any oil, ignored the oil pressure meter, and the engine had seized on him. Lemieux towed him back into the marina, and then found a real mechanic to work on the boat.

Later, the show's producers would film more frequently in Miami, and lean heavily on Davis's marina. Lemieux found himself leasing boats to the show for $1,000 a day through the company, and when they needed an extra for a scene, he was always more than happy to fill in. In fact, when the producers remade the opening sequence to make it look more like it was all filmed in Miami, they included a shot of speedboats racing under the 79th Street Bridge—and one of them was piloted by Lemieux. The show about cops pretending to be drug traffickers had at least one drug trafficker pretending he wasn't one in it at the start of every episode.

Ironically, the only time Lemieux was intercepted by the authorities in that time period was when he was shooting for the show. He recalled that he was on the bay one day when he heard a tremendous noise, and turned around to see a Coast Guard helicopter, no more than thirty feet above the water, checking him out. When he arrived at the marina, law enforcement officers questioned him and searched his boat. Of course, they didn't find anything incriminating since he'd been filming all day.

Things were also changing for Alex. Among the toys he had collected were a couple of private planes. He never used them for smuggling—he was smarter than that—but he did like to drop in on his distributors throughout the country.

He had grown particularly attached to Chicago, enjoying its nightlife and culture so much that he wanted to be part of it. He and Frontera bought and refurbished an old concert venue in the North End called the Riviera Club.

It's not uncommon for traffickers and other gangsters to buy nightclubs and other entertainment facilities. It's largely a cash business—it was essentially all cash back in the day—and Alex realized he could claim huge revenues from the Riviera, even if it lost money. It was an effective way to launder drug money, legitimizing the huge stacks of cash that cocaine trafficking had brought him and keep the IRS off his back. He was fully cognizant that it was them and not the cops who eventually brought Al Capone down.

Besides, Alex loved live music and could essentially afford pretty well any act he wanted to see.

But it wasn't always music that Alex and his Chicago crew wanted to see. Among the popular attractions at the Riviera Club was Jell-O wrestling—a sport in which two bikini-clad women would fight to pin the other in a tub full of the eponymous gelatin dessert.

One of the contestants, in particular, caught Alex's eye. A body-builder, exotic dancer, and part-time model named Nicole Tristani had many of the same qualities as a wrestler that Alex had. She was quick on her feet, spontaneous, and relentless. She was—at least as far as one can be in such a niche activity—a Jell-O wrestling star.

He admired her skills, he liked the way she looked and, when they got to know each other, something clicked. Barely nineteen—not quite old enough to drink in the bars she danced in—and a decade younger than Alex, she started dating him.

She seemed like a good catch for Alex, especially perhaps for the fact that she didn't earn the nickname Nicki the Knife for her Jell-O wrestling prowess. She had a reputation for being as tough outside the Jell-O tub as inside it. She was said to be always carrying a blade and had allegedly gotten into an argument with a man outside Wrigley Field and slashed him across the chest. That kind of fearless ferocity could come in handy, Alex realized.

When she announced she was moving to Miami to be with him, Alex had a little surprise in store for her. Like him, she appreciated motorcycles, so he bought her a Harley-Davidson. But that wasn't quite special enough, so he decided to get it painted hot pink, her favorite color.

John had become the organization's kind of do-anything guy by that time, and he did have some artistic ability, so he was pressed into the task. His first attempt was rejected because it might have been pink, but it wasn't the exact hot pink Alex had specifically asked for. It absolutely had to match the bikini she frequently wore. She even matched her nail polish to it. John eventually found the perfect hue, and even painted her helmet as well.

Nicki was delighted with her gift, and frequently rode her not hard to miss Harley around the area wearing nothing but her hot pink bikini, helmet, and, of course, matching nail polish.

Things were working out for Alex. He was wealthy and happy with Nicki in Miami, and he owned a happening place in Chicago. What was most reassuring to him, though, was his network. Alex was surrounded by friends, most of them from high school or college. He knew them and trusted them. They'd been through the wars together, and they watched each other's backs. It was a tight unit, not unlike Kevin's anti-aircraft platoon at Fort Bliss.

But it was straining. Although they didn't work very often, when they did, they found they had more than they could handle. The loads from the Nerma had grown from 1,500 kilos to 5,500. Nasser David, ever competitive and an inveterate braggart, wanted to ship even more. It wasn't even about the money anymore. He just wanted to be the biggest in the business, even bigger than that upstart from Medellín, Pablo Escobar.

He pressed Alex to get more men to handle the increased workload. He needed another boat, at the very least. The problem was that Alex had tapped out his entire network of wrestlers. He didn't have any left to call. Not anyone he trusted, at least.

So, he leaned on Lemieux, his right-hand man. Lemieux found

someone he knew from the marina. Good guy, strong enough to lift the bales, not to mention an experienced seaman who wouldn't have a problem piloting his boat in international waters in the dead of night. They had lots of friends in common, and seemed to have the right attitude for the crew. Lemieux invited him to the next operation.

He came along, but before he did, he told a few friends in law enforcement what was going down. The guy had become an undercover agent in exchange for leniency after his own trafficking arrest.

Years later, Lemieux said he could hear the Coast Guard plane overhead that night. He knew they weren't in a known flight path, so it made him nervous, prompting him to tell his guys to hurry.

It didn't matter how fast they went, the giant Coast Guard HC-130 Hercules was tracking them from the night sky.

After spotting the small flotilla of "open fishing boats," the crew of the Hercules followed them to a "coastal freighter." Circling over the scene at an altitude that they believed would muffle their already quiet aircraft, they recorded the small boats approaching the Nerma, then the unloading of the cocaine. One of the flight crew shouted: "They've got a party going on down there!"

They couldn't intercept the boats in time, but they could alert police in Florida about their pending arrival.

Despite Lemieux's anxiety, the mission went as planned. As usual, the boats split up and went to separate destinations along Florida's Atlantic Coast.

One of them was unlucky enough to be assigned to Boca Raton, where Detective James Burke was waiting. He had heard rumors that the recent wave of cocaine in South Florida had been brought there by a large ocean-going vessel—some even referred to it as "the Good Ship Lollipop"—but the details about it were sketchy at best.

Even though it was considered an older, more laid-back community, Boca Raton had been soaked by the wave of cocaine that washed over South Florida. Burke—a Chicago native who attended Louisiana State University on a gymnastics scholarship—started his detective career sitting in a pickup truck buying crack from street dealers in front of a hidden camera. But he had moved onto bigger things and on the morning of June 19, 1988, Father's Day—he later told me that drug traffickers always incorrectly think that cops were less active on holidays because they don't like to work them—he received a memo from the Blue Lightning Task Force informing him that smugglers were likely to bring large amounts of cocaine to South Florida in pleasure craft that day.

He alerted his marine unit, which observed a 28-foot Pacemaker (the standard sport fishing boat of the time) named Lassie enter Lake Boca Raton through the very narrow Boca Raton Inlet. The young men they saw aboard didn't look like they were returning from an early fishing trip, so they followed the boat at a discrete distance. If Alex had a cop-spotter boat there, its occupants totally missed Boca Raton police craft shadowing the smugglers.

The boat made its way to a neighborhood called Royal Palms, where plenty of people have docks in front of their multimillion-dollar homes. It then stopped at one of the houses and the smugglers disembarked and started unloading.

The Boca Raton cops arrested them, and called customs and the DEA for help with the cargo. Pretty soon, the Boca Raton canine unit showed up with a German Shepherd (Burke told me that he recalled that his name was Zeus, but he can't be a hundred percent certain), who helped them find a hidden compartment in the cabin's ceiling. In it was hidden 584 kilos of white powder. The dog's reaction gave an initial confirmation that the boat had indeed been transporting cocaine. And the customs guys confirmed it.

The person receiving the cocaine was, Burke told me, "a trust fund baby in his mid-thirties who still lived in his parents' house." It was a very bad time for him to get caught. For much of the

1980s, South Florida was so flooded with cocaine trafficking that the courts and correctional facilities simply could not keep up with them all. According to US attorney Paul Pelletier, in 1988, the nine federal judges in South Florida saw more cases than the fifty-five in Central California, Southern California, Northern California, Southern Texas, Eastern New York, and Southern New York (including New York City) combined. Smugglers who were caught with a few kilos in other cities in America were declared kingpins and going to prison for twenty or even thirty years, but those with the same amount in Miami might not see any jail time at all. There were just too many traffickers for the jails to hold. "You could swing a dead cat on any corner in Miami and hit at least five drug traffickers," Pelletier would later say. Much of the success of the cocaine traffickers in South Florida in the 1970s and early 1980s can be directly attributed to the fact that law enforcement and the judicial system just couldn't keep up with the sheer number of them.

That situation changed a great deal when the United States ratified the Anti-Drug Abuse Act in 1986. As part of the Reagan administration's War on Drugs, it obliged courts to impose mandatory minimum sentencing for drug-related crimes, and it came with sentencing guidelines that judges could not deviate from. The sentencing guideline for a conviction of possessing ten kilos was twenty years with an absolute minimum of ten. Even in formerly permissive Miami, many of Alex's smugglers were looking at spending most of their lives behind bars. And he was responsible for up to 5,500 kilos in a single trip.

To deal with the extra volume of suspects and prisoners, the federal government sent hundreds of millions of dollars to the embattled region to investigate and try drug cases in the region. In the next few years, the US attorney's office in South Florida would double in its number of employees.

In the beginning, Kevin Pedersen (left) and Alex DeCubas were a study in contrasts. Kevin used hard work and an intimate knowledge of wrestling techniques to achieve success while his fellow All-American teammate Alex simply took advantage of brute strength to win championships. *Photos courtesy of Barry Zimbler.*

Cocaine arrived in the United States from Colombia after smugglers developed several complex delivery systems. The distributors engaged Americans, including Alex DeCubas, to arrange for large loads to make their way into the country by air and boat as the War on Drugs escalated. *AP Photo.*

Pablo Escobar, the most famous drug lord, was responsible for supplying an estimated 80 percent of the cocaine smuggled into the United States at his peak. His network included Alex DeCubas, one of the largest homegrown distributors for the US. *AP Photo.*

Operation No Mas was the DEA-led Task Force that included James Burke (above), and had the responsibility of tracking down the local kingpin, Alex DeCubas. Since DeCubas was well-known and vulnerable in the tri-county region of South Florida, Burke and his team relied on counterintelligence to force him on the run. *Photo courtesy of James Burke.*

Creativity was an Alex DeCubas trademark and he was responsible for developing "double-hulled boats" that could transport 1,000 kilos of cocaine per trip. After the confiscation of this boat, DEA task force member James Burke is seen in the hull to show how large of a compartment had been constructed. *Photos courtesy of James Burke.*

On Biscayne Bay, with the rapidly developing, cocaine-driven Miami skyline, Kevin Pedersen (middle) and his fellow DEA agents added to their arsenal. Among their tools were fast boats, which could track down and pursue cocaine traffickers on open water. *Photo courtesy of DEA.*

After being on the run for a dozen years, Alex DeCubas was tracked down in South America and arrested in Colombia. This Policia Nacional booking photo shows Alex and his hair plugs after several journeys, including a connection with Pablo Escobar. *Photo courtesy of DEA.*

Together again on the same team after decades of facing off against each other, Alex DeCubas (left) and Kevin Pedersen discuss strategy before the beginning of a Westminster Christian High wrestling match.

Kevin and Alex exhibit the same intensity as coaches that they displayed as high school teammates and as opposing forces during the War on Drugs. *Photos courtesy of Sandra Padilla Malkus*

As coaches for the Warriors, Kevin and Alex are back together, and sharing an effort to make a difference in the lives of their high school wrestlers. *Photos courtesy of Sandra Padilla Malkus*

Reunions with former Palmetto coach Barry Zimbler (left) allowed his former wrestlers to reminisce about a time when life was simpler and an era in which victories were achieved on a championship wrestling mat. *Photo courtesy of Sandra Padilla Malkus.*

Perhaps even more important than the minimum sentences and the extra manpower from the Anti-Drug Abuse Act was a stipulation in the newly updated Bail Reform Act known as Rule 35. It moved the ability to reduce charges—plea bargaining—entirely to prosecutors. That meant that pleasing a prosecutor was the only way to avoid severe prison time after a drug conviction. And prosecutors only wanted one thing—for small fry to give up the big fish. The game was on. Pelletier and his crew did their best to catch every trafficker they could and offer them leniency in exchange for information on their bosses.

Immediately, the culture among drug smugglers had changed. Knowing that anyone, your closest friend or even your brother, would rat on you in a second to save their own skin and avoid a lengthy prison term meant that nobody trusted anyone anymore.

And prosecutors used it to their advantage. When the arrests were made after the Coast Guard taped the Nerma offloading to the fishing boats, Pelletier offered them all reduced sentences in exchange for giving up their boss. "The same name kept coming up over and over again," he said, "Alex DeCubas."

"They all talked about Alex," Burke told me. "He was the man."

CHAPTER 10

No Mas

Nicki the Knife never wore all that much in Miami. She was hard to miss in her hot pink bikini even when she wasn't on her Harley. So, when she approached two Colombian men who kind of knew her, but weren't exactly sure from where at an outdoor café for help, they were all ears.

She was having problems with her Jet-Ski, she told them, just couldn't get the damn thing started. She knew it had gas, and it had started the day before, but she just couldn't get it to work no matter how hard she tried. Maybe, she told them, it needed a man's touch, and added with a wink that she would make it worth their while.

Smiling, they agreed to help her.

Delighted, she told them to follow her to her garage not far away.

She got on her Harley, and they followed in a Mercedes. She took them down an alley and parked beside a garage. The guys stood behind her as she unlocked the double doors.

She flung the doors open, revealing two men inside with submachine guns pointed at the two Colombians.

Nicki turned back to them and told them that Alex knew they

had stiffed him for two kilos. They would have two weeks to pay him back. If they didn't, they had better be sure to have said their goodbyes and made their peace with God.

The two men told her they understood, and left. Alex received his cash in less than a week.

No blood was shed, but the message was abundantly clear—Alex was not the kind of guy to be messed with.

Burke and Pelletier knew each other well, and when Pelletier mentioned that he was trying to build a case against Alex DeCubas, Burke told him he was as well.

It didn't take long for Burke to put together a task force including his own department, US Customs, the DEA, US Marshals, and other local police forces all for the express purpose of bringing down Alex. He called it Task Force No Mas. *No Mas* is Spanish for "no more," and the idiom was made famous in the United States when Roberto Durán said it when he threw in the towel against Sugar Ray Leonard in their second welterweight championship bout in 1980. Burke even chose a boxing glove for its logo. He would knock Alex out or force him to give up as Durán had.

Alex was oblivious to all that, though. The guys who had been caught had mentioned his name to the interrogators, but they weren't about to let Alex know that. That would have been foolhardy, dangerous even.

He still trusted them. All he knew was that he had lost some of the load to the cops, but that happened from time to time, and he had made plenty of money to cover it. It was one of the hazards of doing business, and he was always prepared.

Even Nasser David was pleased with how much of the giant load had gotten through. He'd broken every record for volume and audacity and gotten paid in full. It would allow him to boast among his peers and maybe he'd finally get as much notice as that punk Escobar if he kept it up.

And he was more than happy to deal with Alex, and he knew that, together, they might be able to get even bigger loads into South Florida. He let Alex know that another huge amount of cocaine—this one in excess of six tons—would be coming in on the Nerma.

Alex had to scramble. He was already down one boat, and the load was even bigger this time. He didn't bother sending Lemieux out this time, though; he just put word out through his group that they needed another captain and the bigger the boat the better.

Before long, a suitable candidate emerged. An ex-Navy man, he told Alex that he could get a recreational trawler which had a much bigger capacity than the little go-fast boats he had been using. The captain had some experience, and he came well recommended.

The drug smuggling community back then was tight-knit. Pelletier used to joke that, although there were at least fifty major drug trafficking organizations in the region, there was really just one because they all knew each other, they all worked for each other, and they all partied together. Word spread quickly if someone could be trusted or not.

The new guy seemed perfect, but he was also an informant. He'd been nailed with a small shipment earlier, and Pelletier offered him leniency in exchange for helping him catch Alex. In fact, after his meeting with Alex, the informant went back to the No Mas Task Force and asked them to rent him a recreational trawler he had promised Alex. He said he needed it because it was a bigger boat than the fishing boats Alex's men had been using, but not big enough to cause major suspicion from law enforcement.

The cops set him up with an appropriate boat, and alerted the Coast Guard that there would be a massive drug drop between Stirrup Cay and Burrow Cay in the Bahamas on the night of July 28, 1989.

The Coast Guard had its own new toy—a helicopter equipped with a forward-looking infrared (FLIR) camera. It was the first device that would allow them to record the operation in real time on video with a high enough quality that it could be used in court as evidence.

Just seventeen days after President George H.W. Bush gave a speech about how America must get tougher on drug smugglers, a Coast Guard cutter moved in on the Nerma. The crew attempted to flee, but they were forced to stop after the Coast Guard's HU-25 Falcon jet dropped a smoke bomb in front of it. Defenseless, the Nerma was boarded by crew from the cutter, and the individual boats were chased down by speedboats armed with .50-caliber machine guns. Agents seized the cocaine and arrested seventeen people. The Nerma was then declared the property of the US federal government. Vanuatu's government did not protest.

At the same time, Burke told me that he was visiting several federal prisons throughout the country to find out more about Alex. Although they knew that he was the one who was coordinating the massive drops, they didn't know where he was getting the coke, nor did they know exactly where he was.

Burke was also gathering evidence to prove that Alex was operating a continuing criminal organization, a charge that would elicit a much stiffer penalty than trafficking alone would, no matter the volume. His work allowed Pelletier to indict Alex, Frontera, Nasser David, and more than two hundred other people involved with the Nerma operation.

Most of them were rounded up in Florida, and Frontera was arrested in Chicago. Nasser David, of course, was off limits, as long as he stayed in Colombia. "It's really frustrating that we cannot get to him in Colombia," said Kenneth Kennedy, a DEA agent working with the No Mas Task Force. "He's in four other indictments. But we'll get him."

Over the next few weeks, scores of arrests were made. One of them, on August 12, 1989, was of the recently unretired Sherouse.

When he was released on bail, he immediately got in touch with Alex. He wanted to give him a heads up. Throughout Sherouse's interrogation, one name kept coming up from the cops and prosecutors over and over again—Alex DeCubas. In fact, they were so interested in Alex, he said, that they offered Sherouse a "get out of jail free" card if he'd give his old friend up.

He didn't take it, at least not right away. Instead, the pair decided that Alex was finished in South Florida. The cops and prosecutors knew who he was, and they probably had enough to put him away for twenty years, but were looking for enough to make it thirty (which actually was the case), and they wouldn't give up until they caught him.

Alex decided that he should leave. "When I was indicted and I was living here, I had everything in my life, but it was either stay here and face a life sentence, or pack up and leave and hope for the best," Alex later said. "So, it was an evolution that got me deeper and deeper into the trade that I was involved in."

Sherouse was hardly the only one talking, and Alex knew it this time. The combined law enforcement forces involved in the No Mas Task Force quickly descended upon the ranch Frontera shared with Alex in Ocala. An extensive search netted the combined force thirteen kilos of coke. Frontera was going to go down hard.

Finally, they tracked down Alex's Miami Beach residence. That search uncovered $6.3 million in cash, but the cops didn't find even a grain of cocaine. Another thing it did not get was Alex himself. He was gone. He hadn't taken much with him, as though he was suddenly tipped off that he knew the cops were on their way, and he was just ahead of them.

But where would he go? He had plenty of friends in Colombia, but it might be too dangerous for him to go there, he thought. Things were hot there, and Nasser David might not actually look too fondly on the fact that Alex was abandoning his vital operation in South Florida.

Instead, Alex decided to go to Brazil because he had once read a story about how Ronnie Biggs, known for the Great Train Robbery in England, had fled there. After his much-publicized getaway, it became well known internationally that Brazil has a policy of not returning foreign fugitives to their home country.

Besides, Rio de Janeiro was a rocking town, he had heard, and he could probably get by with his Spanish and English until he got used to Portuguese. Brazil, he decided, would be his new home. Nicki would come along, of course, and so would Lemieux.

But it presented him with a problem—how would they get there? It was like trafficking in reverse. Flying was out; far too much security had been implemented. Alex decided that he'd have to drive, at least out of the United States.

So, Sherouse bought him a motorhome—a massive Blue Bird Wanderlodge. Alex collected Nicki, Lemieux, and a friend named Tommy O'Donnell, who frequently went on operations with them, to go with him. He tried to recruit Sherouse, but his old friend told him that he had decided to go straight and face the music (in fact, he turned state's witness and gave up just about everybody after Alex had left).

Alex didn't drive straight to Brazil, or even out of the country. Instead, he went on what Burke called a "farewell tour." Alex and his gang traveled all over the United States, reaching out to friends who owed him favors. He had plenty of cash, but what he needed was fake passports and other identification. And he also wanted to see his friends and his beloved country for one last time.

One of his final stops was the Sturgis Motorcycle Rally in South Dakota. Alex had long been a Harley-Davidson enthusiast, as had Nicki, and catching the biggest biker festival in the world seemed like an appropriate way to say goodbye to America. He called Sherouse from the rally, and told him that he loved him and was sad over the fact that if they ever saw each other, he knew it would be because his old pal would be testifying against him in court.

As Burke and his task force began rounding up the remaining members of Alex's crew, the most important question for them had become where's Alex? Nobody knew. Even those who would have gladly given him up had no idea he was on a cross-country tour in a motorhome.

When word got out around the country, tips began to trickle in. Alex's friends and contacts were frequently arrested, and would bargain every bit of information they could to prosecutors. But just as the people chasing Alex were getting information, so was he. His luck held as he continually evaded his pursuers, often with precious little time to spare. Pelletier described his team as being "a hot cup of coffee behind" Alex in several stops around the country, arriving just moments after he had taken off.

The members of the No Mas Task Force did learn, however, that Alex and his crew had been traveling the country by motorhome. As had become par for the course for them, Alex learned about that, and decided to ditch the Blue Bird in San Diego. And, in typical Alex fashion, he replaced it with a limousine he had rented from a company that specialized in catering bachelor parties.

With Alex at the wheel, he, Nicki, Lemieux, and O'Donnell rolled over the border. Their fake passports—Alex's was from the Dominican Republic and gave his name as Juan Vasquez—were good enough for the Mexican border guards. They left the USA in their rearview mirror.

Lemieux was surprised to see Alex stop at a pay phone almost as soon as they were in Tijuana. He might have been on the run, but he didn't stop working. He was calling Jorge Gnecco Cerchar to coordinate the drop-off of two thousand kilos of cocaine from a yacht in the Bahamas.

Gnecco was another major supplier from Northern Colombia and he was very well-connected. Both of his brothers held elected positions in Colombia's government. He had earned a reputation for violence, leading a right-wing paramilitary group—basically his own army—that did his bidding, which included bombings, kidnappings, and assassinations. But he was more than merely violent, he was sadistic. Gnecco would actively take part in torture sessions—which were meted out as punishments more often than they were to learn secrets—and delighted in taking photographs of his victims begging for their lives. Alex said that Gnecco was laughing over the final moments of his victims while he was showing Alex the pictures.

Alex kept driving the stolen limo south along Mexico's Pacific Coast, finally ditching it in a parking lot at Mexico City International Airport.

The quartet boarded an airliner scheduled to arrive in Rio de Janeiro in a few hours, but tensions flared when the plane was stopped on the runway. There was no announcement regarding the delay, but the flight attendants reopened the front door, suddenly, a crew of heavily armed police stormed in.

Alex, Lemieux, and the others were sure it was the end for them and braced for impact. When he opened his eyes, Alex saw that the cops had pulled someone—just two rows ahead of him—out of his seat and dragged him out of the plane.

The captain apologized over the P.A., the door was closed, and Alex and his gang were off to sunny Rio de Janeiro.

Once settled in the city, they acclimatized very quickly. Rio de Janeiro was a lot like Miami South. There was an incredible array of nightlife all focused on Ipanema, one of the most beautiful beaches in the world. Freighters moved in and out of the port at Guanabara Bay, and private boats for anglers and sightseers were plentiful. Cocaine was big there, but the prices were low, and the trafficking networks were already very entrenched and had a reputation for almost indiscriminate violence.

It was a great place, sure, but as the reality of life in Brazil grew on them, while the crew's tension and fear waned, the sadness of never being able to go back to their own country was always present.

It eventually dawned on Alex that all he really needed to run his business was a telephone, so he got in touch with his contacts in Colombia—including Gnecco—and his remaining friends in Miami and got back in business.

The little gang started hanging out at the Lord Jim Pub, which was (and still is), a hangout for English-speaking ex-pats just a few blocks from the sands of Ipanema.

Lemieux even got to meet a locate celebrity—Biggs, who by then made his living by selling T-shirts and renting himself out for lunch dates with British tourists. The two fugitives bonded over common experiences, and he even hosted Christmas dinner in 1991 for the crew.

It was through a friend of Biggs, an Englishman named Tim, that Lemieux learned something he was sure Alex would want to know. Coke was selling for the equivalent of $50,000 a kilo in the United Kingdom. The market in South Florida had been flooded, mostly by Alex, and the price there had fallen to less than $10,000 per kilo.

At first, Alex was skeptical of the idea. He was sure there was no way cocaine sold for that much in England. But if he had buyers there, it made sense to supply them no matter what the price. Life on the run isn't cheap, and neither is Rio.

Alex spoke with Tim and came up with a plan. He bought a sailboat, and Lemieux built some hidden compartments inside it. Alex then arranged for an airdrop of about four hundred kilos in the waters outside Rio from Nasser David's people in Colombia, had Lemieux and the trusty O'Donnell pick it up and sail it to England.

After stopping in the Azores to make arrangements, he piloted his craft to the Isle of Wight off the southern coast of England. At the start of August every year, the island plays host to Cowes

Week, one of the oldest and most popular regattas in the world. Lemieux's craft blended into the more than a thousand sailboats that were there at the same time. He was surprised to learn that the slip he was assigned was right beside that used by the Royal Yacht HMY Britannia, which had carried Prince Edward down to see the competition.

Lemieux was surprised to learn that Tim had neither lied nor exaggerated. At £23,500 a kilo, or just under $48,000 at the time, he had no trouble getting rid of all the product he had brought. His contacts, he said, "begged" for more cocaine.

The only problem was that he couldn't fit that much cash—almost $20 million—into the hidden compartments of his boat. So, he arranged for a freighter that had just dropped off a load of bananas in England and was headed back to Brazil to take back it back for him. He put it in a secure container and told them it was camera equipment. They asked him to sign for it. Unwilling to use his real identity or the name on his fake passport, he chose the first name that popped into his head—Cris Collinsworth. He was pretty sure that it was unlikely anyone in England or Brazil would associate that name with the former University of Florida and Cincinnati Bengals star wide receiver and sports announcer.

But the money still had to be laundered. Alex got in contact with his buddy Felix Chitiva, and he put it through the system the Cali cartel had been using for years.

That meant that it was necessary to make a call to La Jolla, California, to the home of Heidi Herrera. A financial whiz who was celebrated in local media as one of the region's top Hispanic entrepreneurs, behind the scenes she had handled much of the Cali cartel's cash.

The truth was that her real name wasn't Herrera, she wasn't even actually Hispanic, and she wasn't interested in helping the cartels at all. Her name was actually Heidi Landgraf, and she was working undercover for the DEA. She just happened to have learned Spanish while attending medical school in Mexico before she decided to become a DEA agent.

Aware that her blonde hair and blue eyes might make her suspect, the DEA came up with a backstory that her father was a Mexican billionaire smuggler, and her mother was his trophy wife from Austria.

When Lemieux called her, asking if she had any people in England, she gave him a name. But she wanted to let her contact know what was going on, she said, so she asked Lemieux what name he was using in these days. He told her the name on his fake passport—Paul Jeffrey Carpenter. After she hung up, she called into the DEA to tell them that there was an operation going on in England, and they were to keep an eye out for Paul Jeffrey Carpenter.

It didn't take long to track him down in London. He had just rented a posh apartment in a high-rise under the Carpenter name. He later recalled getting in the building's elevator and just as the doors were closing, a hand darted in. As the doors opened, the man who stopped the elevator asked him if he was Paul Jeffrey Carpenter. Lemieux said he was. The man answered: "British Customs, you are under arrest."

O'Donnell went down not long afterward.

Lemieux and O'Donnell were both eventually sentenced to sixteen years in Woolwich Crown Court. The judge told them that they had "contributed to the problems of addiction, damage to health, and poverty and crime" in the United Kingdom. After serving eight years in an English prison, they were sent to Miami. Pelletier was in no mood for deals. Lemieux was sentenced to another twenty years.

And Alex would lose more than just his right-hand man and a trusted lieutenant. Nicki tired of life on the run, and sincerely believed that the cops had nothing on her. She decided to go back home—to Miami, not Chicago—and live in Alex's house with Alex's stuff.

One of those things was a Jeep Cherokee he had bought her—paying more than $20,000 in cash—just before they left. A week after she returned to South Florida, some men followed her out of The Mall at 163rd Street in North Miami Beach. Just as she was getting into the Cherokee, they shouted to her that they were FBI agents. A quick search of the SUV uncovered an orange duffel bag hidden under the driver's seat. In it, was $99,800 in cash. She started cooperating with the agents before she was even in their car.

The gang of four that had left Miami for Rio de Janeiro had been reduced to one. Alex was alone—the one thing he never wanted to be.

CHAPTER 11

Divine Intervention

Kevin could feel the cold metal of the barrel pressed hard against his right temple. Down on his knees, with his eyes shut tightly, teeth clenched, and tears running down his cheeks, he began to squeeze the trigger while thinking, *It's better this way, it's the easy way.*

Then everything went black.

He was sincerely and profoundly surprised when he woke up a few hours later. Confused, he looked around his apartment. The gun was on the other side of the room.

Years later, he assured me that the only explanation was divine intervention. "I believe it was Jesus Christ who knocked the gun out of my hands," he said with the gravity only religion can inspire, "and saved my life."

Kevin had always gone to church and believed in God, like most people of his generation and community, but had never been very devout about it. That changed. He believed that he had been extremely close to taking his own life, only to be spared, and that awoke the spiritual side of him. And like everything else he had ever done in his life, he put his entire heart and soul into it. Kevin had become a man of faith.

What mattered to him after he recovered his wits was why he had been spared. He knew that tens of thousands of people successfully commit suicide every year—he'd even seen it up close in the army—so why, he wondered, was he any different?

He prayed and prayed and examined every detail of his own life up until the point he had a gun pressed against his temple. Through honesty, dedication, sincerity and hard work, Kevin had managed to get everything he had ever wanted. He was a state champion wrestler, he'd graduated from West Point, been an awarded platoon leader in the United States Army, and become a husband and father. He had even stood up to his father, and proved himself worthy.

And then, it was all taken away from him.

The longer he thought about it, the more he realized what had happened to him, and why he felt that his life had received divine intervention. He had skills that could be used to promote what he felt was God's will. If nothing else, Kevin's training, drive, discipline, and spirit had made him one thing—a warrior.

He realized that America's enemy was not the rapidly disintegrating Soviet Union, nor was it Iran or North Korea or any other traditional nation-state. None of them was to blame for what had befallen him and the people around him in recent years.

The enemy, America's enemy, his enemy, was drugs. Drugs took his wife and child away from him. Drugs were directly responsible for him having his command taken away from him. And it was drugs that meant he and everyone he knew couldn't feel safe walking the streets in their own country—something that should be unthinkable in his United States of America.

It had never happened before. When our soldiers went off to Europe, the Pacific, Korea, and Vietnam, he knew they were in danger, but the people at home always felt they were safe. In South Florida at the time, bodies—many of them innocent people in the wrong place at the wrong time—were piling up in the morgue. His country had been invaded. We were losing the war on our own turf, he thought.

And it was all so some two-bit warlord in Colombia could buy another gold-plated Bentley or jewel-encrusted AK-47.

America was at war, not with Colombia, but with the drugs that came from there, and the people who pushed them.

Kevin searched for a way that he could help. He believed deep in his heart he had been saved because he had a purpose on Earth. He had to fight the drug invasion, it was, he believed, God's will.

Eventually, he came across the DEA (it was hardly a household name back then, at least among the law-abiding), and it appealed to him a great deal. "I saw them as . . . kind of paramilitary, a good blending of police and military," he later said. "They saw a lot of action; and, if you wanted to fight the War on Drugs, that's the place to be."

His friends and family agreed. "When I found out that Kevin was considering going into the DEA, it didn't surprise me at all," Gorie expressed to ESPN. "To me, that was the career path that was right in line with his personality—how he looked at life, with strict guidelines, strict requirements, focusing on something that was trying to make our country stronger and better—so it seemed to me a perfect fit."

It didn't happen right away, but Kevin was determined to make it work. And he had no doubt that it would. "So, I started my application process because I knew I was going to have to change my career. I really wanted to make a change with something that God wanted me to do. It was real clear to me that this is what I was supposed to do," he later said. "It was almost like, for me, a cleansing. Getting away from all this crap, and becoming the guy with the white hat."

In the interim, he took a job at a different tire store in Fort Myers, on Florida's Gulf Coast, and began to volunteer as a part-time wrestling coach for a local high school. Even if he wasn't in the DEA yet, he knew he could still do some good in his new community.

Almost two years after he initially applied, Kevin was hired by the DEA in October 1991. It was the fulfillment of another of his childhood dreams—becoming a law enforcement officer.

From that moment, Kevin was different. The depression was gone, and so was all of his dreary talk. He was back to his old self, protecting his country and, this time, he was sure he had God at his side.

He was sent to Roanoke, Virginia, and learned the ropes.

On his very first day at the DEA's Miami-area station, he was surprised to learn that the team of agents across the hall were working on a big case—tracking down and catching the fugitive drug baron Alex DeCubas.

Kevin had figured out by then that Alex was a trafficker, but when he saw the details of the indictments against him, he realized he was not just some amateur operator, but the biggest cocaine supplier in the Southeastern United States ("everything from North Carolina south," Kevin described his territory). Kevin learned that Alex had been indicted—along with Nasser David, who Kevin knew about, and more than two hundred other people—for their parts in a huge cocaine trafficking operation and was a fugitive from justice. "I basically chuckled and shook my head, and said, if there was any doubt . . . it is now over," Kevin recalled. "I can see for myself that my friend was a very strong enemy on the other side of this battle."

The other agents thought it was hilarious that Kevin and Alex had been teammates and best pals in high school. Special agent Kevin Curtis, who led the task force against Alex, remembers that he and the other agents would occasionally engage in some good-natured ribbing over it. "You see Alex lately?" they'd ask. "Tell him to give me a call." Kevin was cool with it, though. He saw the humor in the situation, and offered to help in any way he could.

Exactly how far the cocaine trade had infiltrated the men of his generation became apparent to Kevin a few days into the job. On his way to work, he was served with a subpoena.

He was surprised to learn that Scott Sherouse—who had been on the Palmetto wrestling team and was the same age as Kevin's brother, Mike—had been convicted of cocaine trafficking. The subpoena was to get Kevin to appear in court as a character witness at his sentencing hearing.

The irony of having a straight arrow, freshly minted DEA agent testify to the character of a convicted drug trafficker was not lost on Kevin. He immediately told his boss, David Tinsley, what he had been compelled to do.

Tinsley found it funny, and told Kevin to do what he had to do. Kevin admitted it was more than a little embarrassing that his first time testifying in court would be on behalf of a dealer, but Tinsley assured him it was nothing to worry about. Sherouse, he had learned, had turned into a cooperating witness and was giving up everyone he knew (although he genuinely did not know where Alex had gone), so the desire to get him a long prison term had largely evaporated. But Tinsley couldn't help joining in the fun. "Just be sure the next time you're in court," he told Kevin, "that it's on our side."

Kevin did take the stand, but had little to say.

He would not be dissuaded by minor distractions, though. "I wanted to go right to the top," he said. "I wanted to take out the biggest drug dealers there were—the Colombians."

It didn't start out that way. Like any other large organization, the DEA starts its new recruits out small. "I knew some people from the Homestead area and started working cases with the police department there," Kevin said. "They were what I call little cases, a kilo or two kilos of coke. That's where I learned how you set up a case. How you arrest a guy. I was out weekly at night doing cases, March 1992 until early 1993. About a year and a half later, I became a lead case agent."

Being in the DEA in the early '90s was a lot like being in the army in 1980—absolutely out of step with just about everything and everyone that was going on in South Florida. Although he was relieved that he didn't have to wear a suit and tie that often, Kevin's short hair and modest clothing budget stood out in well-coiffed, Armani-draped and gold-trimmed Miami. "I couldn't walk into a bar without being patted down for a wire," he said. He knew they were joking, but he also knew there was some truth to it. Just as often, when he'd enter a bar, he'd watch as two or three other guys—all wearing the standard trafficker uniform—would walk out.

Among the men of South Florida in his generation, it seemed to him that he was actually in the minority by not being in the drug business. If Alex was the region's kingpin and Sherouse was also a trafficker, how was Kevin to know who among his old friends handled drugs and who didn't? To him, they all certainly looked the part. And he'd see their names—guys he wrestled with, even guys he had looked up to—when he went through the DEA reports and databases. "These are people that I have a very good suspicion are involved in something they shouldn't be involved in," he said. "But that's the way it was—South Florida . . . it's a sad, sad indictment of our generation."

And they would always ask, "How's Alex?" or "Ya heard from Alex?" It wasn't funny when they said it. They didn't want Alex to get caught. They considered him some sort of folk hero. Kevin wished he could tell them what Alex really was, what he had read in the reports back at the office. But he held his tongue. Leaking such information could jeopardize the case and, potentially, his career.

But Kevin never got over that feeling. Even if they knew about Alex, and what he had done, it probably wouldn't matter to them—it was the bigger the better with those guys. Kevin could never understand why people would idolize a criminal.

He did know, however, that Alex was not going to stop and he understood why. "Alex and people like him, they're wrestlers, who are obsessive-compulsive," he said later. "They're never going to have enough. When they start making that money, they probably didn't even know how much money they even had. But they weren't going to stop. They won't stop. I'm sure it's a total addiction." He knew because he felt that way himself. "Just like me . . . it was an adrenaline high," he said. "To get this guy, take their money, I mean, you're dying to make an arrest. You're dying to put the handcuffs on the guy. We loved taking them down to the concrete. That's an adrenaline high."

He even recalled how his wrestling training helped him in his job. He was part of a team protecting an undercover agent who was investigating a retired New York City cop who moved to Opa-locka, Florida, to start dealing. Kevin's team followed the undercover agent, who was going to make a deal inside the guy's house. That's against DEA protocol because the other officers can't see what's going on and can't lend aid very quickly, and the deal went bad almost immediately. The suspect was a former cop, so the DEA guys were sure he'd have a gun, and the experience to know how to use it.

Realizing he had been set up, the retired cop and an accomplice fled. The accomplice jumped into a car and tried to run the undercover agent over. He had his gun out, and fired shots at the driver.

The original suspect fled on foot. Kevin ran him down, and brought him to the concrete in the middle of Sharazad Boulevard. When he tackled the dealer, he felt a gun in his waistband. Most law enforcement officers would have pulled their guns at that point, but not Kevin. He knew he could immobilize the much bigger suspect and disarm him even before help arrived.

But there was a problem. Opa-locka was almost entirely populated by African-Americans. It didn't look good for a white cop to be seen manhandling a black suspect in the middle of a quiet residential street. Making matters worse, shots had been fired in the neighborhood—which meant the operation had to be investigated by higher-ups—and, even more damning, no drugs had been found on the suspect, or in his house.

Things did not look good for Kevin, in particular. Recent images of the Rodney King beating in California were fresh in many people's memories. Things had been tense in many African American neighborhoods for cops. Kevin recalled that when they showed up in certain areas, kids would warn the entire community that the cops had arrived by yelling "9-1-1!"

If there were no drugs to be found at the scene, it would look like Kevin was beating an innocent man who simply tried to escape police persecution.

Kevin and the other cops there—all of whom were white, except for the undercover agent who led them there—searched frantically for any hint of cocaine. Just as they were prepared to give up, a little boy approached Kevin, and pointed up.

Kevin turned his head to where the kid had pointed. There it was, up on the roof, a plastic Publix shopping bag.

Kevin climbed up on the roof and retrieved the bag. Inside, were three kilos of cocaine. The suspect had swung it up there while fleeing, and had nearly gotten away with it.

Kevin gave the coke to his supervisor, then returned to the kid. He only had ten bucks in his pocket, but he handed it to the kid and thanked him.

In time, the qualities Kevin brought to the DEA impressed his coworkers. His God-and-country attitude was obvious, and Kevin quickly won the unalloyed trust of everyone he worked with. In a job full of temptations—agents handled literally tons of cash and cocaine, and some fell victim to one or the other—Kevin was the one everybody knew was going to do everything by the book, without fail. If you sent Kevin to go get a million dollars, he would deliver a million dollars every single time. His boss, Tinsley, would later say, "Kevin is the type of guy you'd want your daughter to marry, and the type of guy you hope your son would never have to fight."

Still a man of deep faith, Kevin always carried a bible in his car's glove compartment. He'd offer it, free of charge, to anyone he arrested.

Once Kevin got to work in earnest, he started producing. The DEA's Miami Region headquarters is in Doral, just west of the airport. When Kevin was there, they used to have a board on which they would put up agents' statistics for busts and seizures, as if they were baseball players. Though he started at the bottom, before long, Kevin's name was always at or near the top.

He just seemed to have a knack for the job. Kevin began his career by riding along with officers of the Miami Police Department. He learned from them how to tell a real trafficker from a wannabe in Armani and, more important, how to talk with people to gain their trust and get their information.

One of the things he learned right away is that almost all deals in the South Florida region took place in restaurants. It made sense. They are public places that are usually designed so that people can have private conversations without the fear of being overheard. One agent told me they preferred open-concept places, so that it would be easier to tell if they were being followed or recorded. All restaurants in those days had pay phones, which were (at the time) a necessary tool of the trade. And the businesses themselves were often frequently owned by traffickers or people sympathetic to them because they were ideal facilities for money laundering.

While plenty of deals went down at the fancy places near the ocean, Kevin learned about one unlikely seeming hot spot—Denny's. "Just about any Denny's close to the airport was a forum for [covert] recordings over the years," said Steven Chaykin, who was an assistant US attorney at that time. "Virtually all the major undercover investigations involving importation of marijuana or cocaine inevitably had meetings in or around a Denny's."

And it was at a Denny's that Kevin became aware of Vinicio Avegnano. He owned an ice cream company up in Hialeah, and he supplied frozen treats to a number of restaurants in South Florida, so he knew basically everybody who was anybody in the food service business.

And he had gotten into trouble at the start of 1993. The DEA had learned that he had been distributing more than just spumoni and mint chocolate chip on his rounds. With cocaine trafficking charges hanging over his head, Avegnano agreed to help the DEA bring down bigger fish. He would act as an undercover agent, secretly recording conversations with a more important dealer. He told Kevin he knew just the right guy.

Café Sci Sci was a fancy, upscale Italian restaurant in the trendy Brickell neighborhood. A few tourists dropped in from time to time, but its clientele was made up mainly of Miami's local movers and shakers—and, at that time, that meant traffickers.

Avegnano knew the guy who called himself the general manager of Café Sci Sci, even though he believed that Giovanni Tummolillo was secretly the restaurant's owner as well. Good guy, very generous, he assured Kevin, very well connected. He told Kevin that Tummolillo dealt, and that the restaurant was always full of traffickers, many of whom worked for the big boss.

Kevin, of course, wanted not just to catch Tummolillo, and he also wanted to shut the restaurant down. That would send a message to the traffickers that their safe spaces were not as safe as they believed.

Avegnano went to Café Sci Sci and began to hang out with Tummolillo. After a feeling-out period, Avegnano told him that he had some friends in Italy who would love to get their hands on some luxury items that were either unavailable or ridiculously expensive over there.

Tummolillo agreed that they could make a few bucks that way.

Eventually, their conversation—as many did at the time in Miami—turned to the subject of cocaine. Avegnano asked his friend if he could score him any; you know, for personal use. Tummolillo smiled and said his brother-in-law could, no problem. Avegnano asked him how long it would take. Tummolillo said it would be maybe a half an hour.

After hashing out the details of how much coke he needed and how much Avegnano would pay, Tummolillo walked over to Café Sci Sci's pay phone and called his brother-in-law.

About thirty minutes later, Tummolillo pointed out the window at a Mercedes-Benz that was pulling up in front of the restaurant. "That's him," he told Avegnano.

The undercover agent then walked out of the restaurant and into the car. The brother-in-law drove a couple of blocks up Southeast 10th Street and pulled into a coffee shop parking lot. Stopped, but with the engine and air-conditioning still running, he exchanged a little bag of white powder for a wad of cash, then he drove Avegnano back to Café Sci Sci.

That deal allowed Kevin to get a warrant to listen in on conversations within Café Sci Sci. By November 1993, he had enough evidence to make a series of arrests, including that of Tummolillo, as the restaurant proved to be something of a shipping department for several operators to send cocaine from Florida to Italy, where prices were much higher. Although unable to gather enough evidence to have a strong case to say that Tummolillo was handling any cocaine, Kevin's argument against him was that he was what law enforcement calls a "silent boss"—someone who allows drug deals to go on in his presence, and gets a cut, without always taking an active role in the transactions.

Tummolillo's defense team, led by Richard Sharpstein, tried to discredit Avegnano and his DEA handlers, including Kevin, pointing out that the deal they made would reward him with one-quarter of any assets seized and confiscated after conviction, including Café Sci Sci and even Tummolillo's house.

Although the prosecutors, Robert Lehner and William Shockley, could not prove that Tummolillo had ever handled any cocaine or received any cash, they had enough evidence that he was aware of the dealing at his restaurant, and he was convicted on seven conspiracy charges by US District Judge Lenore Nesbitt.

When Kevin attended Tummolillo's sentencing hearing in March 1996, he—and the rest of the courtroom—were shocked when the convicted man blatantly threatened him, his new wife, his son, and his two daughters, like a gangster from an old Hollywood movie. It certainly did not help his cause when it came to leniency, and it made Kevin something of a celebrity around the headquarters at Doral.

Getting remarried was a big part of turning his life around. His new wife, Michele, was a Texas A&M graduate who had worked in the pharmaceutical industry (selling legal drugs, one might say). He met her at a Wednesday night bible study group at his church. More important, she shared his views on faith and what was actually important in life.

Kevin had won custody of Danny from Betty, and he was turning out to be very much like his old man—conservative, religious, polite, and soon expressing a desire to go to West Point. Michele also had two more children with Kevin, daughters Lauren and Krista.

Kevin had come a long way in the time between having a gun pressed up to his head—ready and willing to end it all—and when a big-time drug dealer threatened his family in court. Kevin didn't laugh it off, but he knew that he was more than capable of protecting his family from guys like Tummolillo. He had found himself. Even more than he did with the army, Kevin realized that he was doing the right thing, doing what he was meant to do. Kevin was fighting the good fight.

CHAPTER 12

The Great Escape

Alex walked out of the Lord Jim Pub and down the street toward Ipanema. He was going to hang out on the beach, but he first stopped at a pay phone to call his contacts in Miami. He was checking in on the four tons of cocaine they were moving for Gneccho—the same deal he called about from the pay phone in Tijuana.

Everything went off without a hitch, he was told.

It hadn't, though. All of it had been picked up and taken to the same warehouse Alex had used for years. The yacht captain, who was an informant, was chosen to stand guard over the stash overnight.

He was sitting in the warehouse, reading, when the front door popped open. Certain it was the police, he calmly put his book down and stuck his hands in the air.

It wasn't the cops. The contact Alex spoke with on the phone to coordinate the operation walked in with four other guys that the captain recognized from Alex's crew. They pointed assault rifles at his head. On a signal from the boss, one of them punched the captain in the face, knocking him down. The armed men continued to punch and kick him until he stopped moving. The first puncher then tied him up and gagged him. He watched, helpless, as they made off with eight hundred kilos. Even at just $10,000 a kilo, that was an easy $8 million.

There's a truism in the drug trafficking business that the only way to keep your people from robbing you blind is the constant threat of violence. But Alex didn't have that anymore. The last time someone stole from him, he had Nicki lure them into a garage and had his men threaten them with execution. But what did he have now? Nicki was gone, and the guys he would have used for muscle were the very ones stealing from him. If they wanted to take the cocaine for themselves, how was he going to stop them all the way from Brazil?

But Alex didn't know that. Again, he trusted them. They didn't have the contacts in Colombia, he did. Without him, he believed, there would be no coke. Besides, with Lemieux behind bars, his operations in Miami had to work or he'd have nothing.

It was one of those Colombian contacts that called him in Brazil. One of Gnecco's lieutenants told him that he was needed in Bogotá. Alex wanted to know why. The guy told him he just had to "go over some numbers," no big deal, he said, standard accounting stuff.

Alex agreed, and drove to Bogotá. He met his contact in a small apartment in the suburbs. As Alex sat down on the couch in the living room, armed men burst out of the bedroom and kitchen. They tied him up, put a hood over his head, and tossed him into a waiting van.

When the hood was taken off, Alex found himself in a large house, part of a compound, high up in the mountains. It was surrounded by a tall fence that Alex would later learn was topped with broken glass.

Alex was frog-marched inside the house. He was taken to an office, where he saw Gnecco behind a desk, and two more armed men behind him.

After Alex was seated across from him, Gnecco pounded on the desk and demanded to know what had happened to the load.

Alex told him he didn't know what he was talking about—and he really didn't because he still naïvely trusted his friends in Miami, and it did not occur to Alex that they would steal from him.

After much arguing, Gnecco pounded the desk again and gave Alex an ultimatum: He could leave the compound once he came up with the $25 million he said he owed him for the lost coke. Then he left.

Alex didn't know what to do. He didn't have $25 million, and with Lemieux behind bars and his Miami connections in what he eventually realized was full betrayal mode, he settled in for a long stay and the hope that he could either come up with a plan or that the infamously ruthless Gnecco would have a change of heart.

With Alex inside the house were a group of armed men who worked in eight-hour shifts. At first, they watched every move he made, generally with their guns pointed at him at all times. But, since Alex was still Alex, he charmed them easily and the compound took on a relaxed, even fraternal mood. Before long, he was playing chess or sports with them, and even having the odd beer. He might have been their prisoner, but he was also one of the guys.

Gnecco would drop by from time to time, to see how Alex was doing, and to give him a chance to make up for the missing 800 kilos or to raise the $25 million he claimed it was worth. He'd drive up, and allow Alex to call Miami from the phone in his car—back then, a brick-sized mobile phone was still the height of technology in Colombia—to try to track down the guy who stole the coke from him.

But it was in vain. Nobody was giving him up. Why would they? With Alex effectively and permanently out of South Florida, how could he either entice or threaten them? Stuck in Colombia, Alex had neither a carrot nor a stick.

He knew that Gnecco would not have unlimited patience with him. He sincerely liked Alex, but it was costing him money to keep him alive. They both knew that the situation couldn't last forever. Alex could not stop thinking about how delighted Gnecco had been while showing him the photos he took of his execution victims back in happier times.

He had to make a better plan.

As he got to know the guys guarding him, Alex found out they shared a common interest to the point of addiction—something he knew he could take advantage of. Once they began to believe that Alex wouldn't cause them any trouble, they started watching telenovelas—hyper-melodramatic TV serials not unlike North American soap operas. They would gather around the living room TV, put their weapons down, open a few beers and watch the fictional intrigues unfold. It was all cool as long as Alex watched along with them.

One night, however, he didn't. As they gathered in the living room, he waited just behind a slightly ajar bedroom door for them to get engrossed in the plot, without noticing he wasn't with them. Just after the opening of the second act, Alex—still a better athlete than any of them—exploded out the door, through the house, and out the front entrance. With his old leather jacket torn in half and wrapped around his hands, he climbed the fence and made his way over the broken glass. Once at the top, he vaulted over and found himself sliding down a gravelly cliff on his behind.

When he got to the bottom, he made his way to a dirt road and ran as far as he could from the compound. Before long, he came across a car. It was just Alex's luck that it was a taxi looking for a fare. He hopped in and told its driver to take him to Chitiva's house in Medellín, more than five hundred miles away, up in the mountains. He assured the driver that his friend would pay him handsomely when they arrived.

The driver had some qualms. It wasn't the distance, or the obvious fact that the filthy, sweating man in the back seat of his car was being chased by someone, it was the fact that Medellín had turned into a war zone. The Colombian government had backed down from the cartel kingpins, and given in on its primary demand—ending its extradition treaty with the United States. That pacification plan backfired, however. Without the fear of time behind bars in American prisons, the drug lords simply increased their pressure on the government and one another. Pablo Escobar's short and embarrassing stint in Congress had led to open combat between him and forces loyal to President César Gaviria Trujillo. The other cartel leaders, assuming Escobar's forces had been severely weakened, moved in and violently tried to take over Medellín. The result was a constant state of violence that made the Miami drug trafficking scene look like a child's tea party.

Alex wasn't afraid. All he wanted to do was put distance between Gnecco and himself as quickly as possible. And with nothing left for him in Miami, and little reason for him to return to Rio de Janeiro with Nicki, Lemieux, and O'Donnell gone, his best bet, he believed, would be to work within Colombia with Chitiva—at least until he got back on his feet.

Of course, Chitiva also wanted him back as his partner. Everyone in cocaine business knows that getting the drug in Colombia isn't tough, and selling it in the United States is simple. The big problem is getting it there, and Alex had proven, time and time again, that he could do it.

Once Alex was settled in Medellín at the end of November 1991, Chitiva took him to meet with Luis "Nicky" Ramirez, who worked for Fernando "the Wolfman" Galeano, one of Escobar's most prominent lieutenants. Through Ramirez, Galeano offered the pair two thousand kilos as a trial run.

Alex got back on the phone with his guys in Miami. They had

been shortsighted. Without Alex, there had been no more flow of cocaine for them. They never gave up the guy who had stolen from Alex, but they did agree to go back to work for him.

Three days after the meeting with Ramirez, Alex had five hundred kilos of cocaine in a small private plane headed for the Bahamas.

How times had changed. American Alex—who had made his name originally as a rip artist, robbing dealers for their drugs, cash, and weapons—had become a trusted trafficker, using the time-tested methods and routes pioneered ages ago by the Colombians. While at the same time, many of the biggest Colombian bigwigs, including Galeano and even Escobar himself, became far less interested in actual trafficking, preferring to make their money through extortion, kidnapping, and, of course, robbing fellow traffickers.

And then the unthinkable happened: Escobar gave himself up. Well, that's not exactly true. He had made a deal with the government under which he would go to prison—but only if he was allowed to make the rules. That meant that he was the only prisoner in La Catedral (the Cathedral), a comfortable mansion that he had designed with a soccer field, a giant dollhouse for his daughter, a wet bar, a hot tub, and a contemplative waterfall. Escobar was allowed to pick his own "guards" from among his men, and the government was not allowed to come within miles of what people were calling "Club Escobar" without his express permission. Friends and business associates, however, could come and go as they pleased (or as Pablo instructed).

One of the people who received an invitation for an audience with the man himself at La Catedral was Chitiva. Escobar told him that he knew all about him and Alex and said that that they were "good people." Chitiva was surprised that Escobar didn't want to negotiate or even tell him the details of their deal. Instead, he just told him that "the organization will take care of" them.

It had become a tradition that anyone visiting Escobar in La

Catedral offer a cash tribute to the man regarded as king of the narco-traffickers. Too small a gift, and you could end up buried in one of Escobar's many private cemeteries. Chitiva left behind $150,000 in American hundred dollar bills.

Things were looking up again for Alex. With Chitiva's help, he would get cocaine through Ramirez, through Galeano from the mighty Pablo Escobar himself. It would be his job to get it from the Bahamas to Florida, and the money would come flowing back to Colombia like the pipeline of almost unlimited cash he had enjoyed when he was still living in Miami.

It was a productive situation that lasted for a few months. In July 1992, Escobar's men kidnapped Galeano and another lieutenant, Gerardo Moncada, and brought them to La Catedral. Because of some irregularities in their accounting, Escobar had them, their brothers, and their accountants tortured and killed. They were torn to pieces, and what remained of them were burned on the property's many outdoor cooking grills, sending a terrifying cloud of reeking smoke over Medellín.

When an American news team found out and broadcast the story, the Colombian government rescinded its participation in the original deal with Escobar, demanded he surrender himself and La Catedral, and submit to being held in an ordinary maximum-security prison. Escobar simply walked out of La Catedral's back gate with his friends and went into hiding.

He wasn't out of business. He had only lost his fortress and his grudgingly provided government protection.

But his flight from La Catedral made Escobar look weak, and there was no shortage of people who wanted him gone, ranging from the DEA, the Colombian government, both right-wing and left-wing insurgency groups and especially rival dealers. Some of them formed a loose association known as Los Pepes—the name was derived from the phrase "Perseguidos por Pablo Escobar" (those who have been persecuted by Pablo Escobar). It was founded by Cali Cartel boss Hélmer "Robapapas (Potato Thief)" Herrera Buitrago after some of Escobar's men tried to assassinate him on September 25, 1990. He was sitting in the stands of a soccer stadium in Candelaria when twenty men dressed as police and soldiers opened fire on the crowd. Eighteen people died, but Herrera emerged unscathed and swore revenge.

Los Pepes had a plan for getting rid of Escobar, even though they couldn't yet find him. They would approach anyone who worked for Escobar, kill them, take all of their drugs and cash and pass along any useful information they could get from them to the Colombian authorities. Suddenly, nobody wanted to work for Escobar. As he lost his people, Escobar lost his revenue and power. And as the Colombian authorities—who had reinstated their much-feared extradition treaty with the United States—and DEA learned more about him, the noose around his neck tightened.

Technically, Alex and Chitiva worked for Escobar. But since Escobar had tortured and killed their boss, Galeano, Los Pepes did not hold their association with the boss against them and welcomed them into their fold with open arms. They could continue to deal, but anything they knew or heard about Escobar and his whereabouts had to be reported back to Los Pepes. Any hint that they were helping to hide Escobar would mean an immediate death sentence with no chance at appeal.

Information from Los Pepes helped the Policía Nacional de Colombia (Colombian National Police) track Escobar to a small apartment in Los Olivos, a blue-collar section of Medellín. As they burst in, Escobar and his trusted right-hand man, Alvaro "El Limón" (the Lemon) de Jesús Agudelo fled out a back door. They were shot and killed while fleeing along the rooftop of an adjoining building while trying to make it to a nearby alley.

Things changed in Colombia after Escobar's demise. Although

Los Pepes no longer had a singular goal, the associations they had made allowed everyone in the trafficking game to work together with fewer restrictions.

Alex, in effect, became a freelancer, moving cocaine for several different suppliers to buyers all over the world.

But it was anything but automatic. The Cali Cartel—which had been allies of Escobar's Medellín Cartel until Pablo started entertaining grandiose thoughts of controlling the whole country—still held some animosity toward anyone who worked with Escobar. When Alex arrived for a meeting, he was greeted by some tough-looking armed men, who did not appear to be happy to see that he had arrived.

Without much in the way of small talk, he was handed two things, a double shot of *aguardiente*—the anise and sugarcane-based liquor preferred in the mountainous southern part of Colombia over the north coast's fondness for rum—and a soccer goalkeeper's jersey.

They escorted him behind their main building to a soccer pitch. Alex hadn't played soccer in years—it was never one of his favorite sports—he was approaching middle age, had gained quite a few pounds and had chronically sore knees, but he knew he had to give it at least an honest try if he was going to get out of the area alive. He downed his aguardiente, motioned for another, and threw on the jersey.

They took shots at him for two hours, but none of them could get a ball past him. His knees might be complaining and his belly jiggling, but he was still Alex.

As the test drew to a close, Alex was surrounded by his new friends, and became the recipient of backslaps, handshakes, more aguardiente, and even a few hugs.

All was forgiven. He knew he was free to do business with members of the Cali Cartel.

Learning from Lemieux's mistakes, Alex went back to servicing high-dollar buyers in England. He even sent a freighter through the Caribbean island of St. Lucia to Greece for vacationers, mainly British, there.

He also vowed not to repeat his own mistakes. His operation in the United States had broken down because the people he worked with up there no longer feared him. In the drug trafficking game, without fear, there is no respect and without respect, Alex learned, people don't mind walking all over you.

So, he went back to the United States several times, as a show of strength, despite being a wanted fugitive. He would fly from Colombia to Mexico, then rent or even buy a car and drive over the border.

It was, of course, very risky; but Alex was still Alex. His confidence in his abilities never wavered. And it's not like there weren't close calls. He was stopped for a traffic violation in Tennessee, and the state trooper there was fooled by a fake passport. Alex took his ticket and paid the fine by mail before he left (he didn't want them to investigate any further). On another trip, he was literally face-to-face with an off-duty officer from the Palm Beach Sheriff's office. He seemed to recognize him, but it wasn't until the officer got back to the office the next day that it dawned on him that he was just a few feet away from the notorious fugitive Alex DeCubas. It was on one of these covert trips that Alex ran into an utterly shocked Coach Zimbler at a University of Miami Hurricanes football game.

As daring as he was, Alex did not get caught on his furtive forays back to the United States. And he wasn't without his close calls in Colombia, either.

Alex liked to tell one particular story about how he and a friend were sailing back to Colombia in a small boat with $6 million in US currency aboard. Alex was looking out a porthole when he saw another boat approaching. It was from Migración Colombia, the nation's border patrol.

Alex knew how those guys worked. They wouldn't arrest him and his pal; they would kill them, dump their bodies and keep the cash for themselves. One of them would probably take the boat home as well.

Immediately, Alex had an idea. His friend, who was piloting the boat, was Dutch and had a habit of not wearing much clothing when the weather allowed. As the patrol boat approached, Alex hastily handed him a glass of wine and told him to "act as gay" as he could.

The sight of the tall, blonde man, wearing nothing but a white thong, carrying a glass of wine, mincing about and waving was enough, Alex claimed, to put the border patrol guys off. They veered off course, and Alex and his friend made it back to their home port without any further incident.

Alex did actually get arrested in Colombia. But by the time the US authorities arrived at the station where he was being held, they were told that it was a case of mistaken identity, and that the man they had believed was Alex DeCubas was actually a legitimate businessman from the Dominican Republic who had no ties to the drug trade. Alex later revealed that it was actually two fistfuls of US currency that led to the misunderstanding being taken care of so quickly.

*   *   *

It was a period when Alex was living large; he had become a caricature of himself. He had more money and time than he ever imagined. He later said that he felt naked if he left one of his houses with less than $10,000 in his pockets.

And nobody dared threaten or even bother him. In the weeks between shipments, he could be found riding his airplane-loud Harley-Davidson—with an open bottle of Jack Daniel's between his legs and a girl or two on the back—through the streets of Medellín either to or from one of the five houses he owned in the area. The police never had the nerve to bother him, and neither did anyone else.

Surprisingly, one of the suppliers he worked for was Gnecco. In the time that had passed since his daring escape, Gnecco had forgiven Alex, even laughed about the whole thing. Alex, he had decided, was far too valuable a transporter to lose over 800 lousy kilos.

They actually began to get close. Gnecco would drop by one of Alex's places for a drink and a chat. If Alex was at one of Gnecco's lavish parties, he'd be introduced as "my star transporter." After Alex and Chitiva moved a few thousand kilos for him, Gnecco told him the old debt had been effectively repaid.

But as Alex began to pile up stacks of cash and live more brazenly, Gnecco had an idea (the kind only he could have).

As Alex was driving his BMW 750iL in downtown Medellín, his path was blocked by a small van. As Alex stopped and honked his horn, men burst from the van and pointed guns at him. Alex looked back and saw that he was boxed in by another van, also with gunmen.

He had been kidnapped again. The men tossed him in the back of the first van, tied him up and drugged him.

When he woke up, he was in a small cottage. He was chained by one of his ankles to a small bed. His chain was long enough so that he could stand and walk around. There was a barred window where he could see the sea (he didn't know it, but it was the Caribbean) and a bucket for his primary needs.

Although Alex was still in the dark, Chitiva figured out what had happened. He drove up to Gnecco's headquarters in Santa Marta to talk to his men. He told them they had made a horrible mistake.

They didn't have to kidnap Alex because the old debt had been paid.

But they knew that. Gnecco had ordered Alex grabbed and they were not at liberty to say why.

Chitiva then went to Gnecco himself and asked what was going on. After all, they had not stolen from him or cheated him, and Alex's debt had been called off. Gnecco said he knew all that, but he had also heard Alex was making tons of money and, frankly, he just wanted some of it.

Chitiva was flabbergasted. After some tense and very tactful negotiation, Gnecco agreed to release Alex for $500,000 in cash. Chitiva paid him and Alex was freed.

Not long after, Alex's girlfriend became pregnant. There were complications, and she went into labor six weeks early. Alex called an ambulance, but his baby just wouldn't wait. By the time the paramedics arrived, Alex was already beginning to guide his son into the world, but they just finished the job for him.

It was a boy. And, like Kevin's son, he was named Daniel, better known as Danny. Because of his premature birth, Danny was very small at first and Alex gave him the nickname "Tiny." The name stuck between the two of them, even though Danny showed no ill effects from his premature birth and grew into a large and healthy boy.

Danny would later tell me that he had a very pleasant childhood in Medellín, with all the toys and friends a kid could want. Of course, that was because his dad, the man he knew as Juan Vazquez, was making so much money with his job as an engineer.

CHAPTER 13

The Twinkie

While Alex was still in Colombia, the rest of the old Palmetto wrestlers would get together every once in a while. They'd hash over the old days and they would trade opinions about what they thought the latest set of Panthers looked like while catching up on each other's lives.

Wrestlers are like that. When it gets in your blood, it usually stays with you for life. And these guys had a common bond—fondness and gratitude for Coach Zimbler—that helped keep them together. "Whenever you have a wrestling coach that you spend a lot of time with, you develop a relationship that is close to a parental relationship," Dom Gorie later told reporters. "Coach Zimbler was held in high esteem and everyone, including myself, respected what he said and tried to do their best to meet those expectations. We were better young men because of him."

They had been a largely successful group. Gorie, who had become an astronaut, was something of the star of the group, but even he was impressed when he saw Kevin walk in. It was pretty clear what he did for a living. Everywhere he went, he had a pair of active two-way radios clipped to his outfit and a couple of weapons, one on his belt and another usually strapped to his calf.

And he was no ordinary DEA agent. Kevin had distinguished himself, winning the administrator's Award of Honor, the highest commendation the DEA could give one of its agents—twice.

It wasn't just that he was another tough guy making busts. Kevin wasn't the Hollywood version of a top DEA agent. Actually, what made him special was the opposite part of his character. A huge part of a successful law enforcement officer's career—especially when it comes to drug trafficking cases—lies in getting people to talk. It's also the hardest part of the job for most agents. But it came naturally to Kevin. David Tinsley, Kevin's boss, said that he was an especially effective officer (even calling him a "prototype agent"), because he could put witnesses and suspects at ease simply by relating to them. He could penetrate any bullshit detector, and come out clean. Kevin, Tinsley said, could find the good in any person, and sincerely believed he could use that connection to form a bond, which often resulted in people cooperating with him. "Kevin had a real, genuine ability to translate that he cared for a person," Tinsley said. "And, by virtue of that, the person would give one hundred percent back to him." To the cynical, it might sound like a scam, but it wasn't. Kevin was just that guy.

Because of his great ability to get people to talk, Kevin was put in charge of a team that investigated high-dollar money laundering cases. Since the time of the rumrunners in the 1930s, federal agents have found that the best way to catch the kingpins of organized crime was to examine their financial dealings intensely. But it's not just numbers. A good agent such as Kevin could get people to talk about which bar had two sets of books, which assets weren't real, and who really owned things that were registered under someone else's name.

While it was probably the most effective way to bring down the big traffickers, few in the DEA wanted to do it. In the administration's macho culture, most agents were after the guns-out jobs, getting the bad guys to drop to the ground, while the agents paraded bricks of cocaine or mountains of cash in front of the media.

Kevin, however, took to the idea of following the money immediately because he understood its value. "Traffickers are in business to make money . . . and they can lose some when it gets seized, and that hurts them," he said. "You can take the drugs, but when you take their money, you're really hurting them."

It was a different time. Guys were, as Tinsley pointed out, walking into Ferrari dealerships and buying cars with $150,000 in fives. Smart agents knew that following the money trail would get them to the big players.

Kevin began cultivating cooperating witnesses all over the eastern half of the United States. He knew that many people involved in money laundering had no idea what they were doing was illegal—they sincerely believed they were simply doing business and they had nothing at all to do with the drug trade. They were, of course, wrong. And once they were arrested and facing the cold shock of long prison sentences, they were more prepared to bargain to save their own freedom at the expense of others. Still, more people would come to him because they were desperate for cash—the DEA offered handsome rewards for information, and still does—and a few even came forward simply because they wanted to "do the right thing."

But the best ones were the guys who were caught red-handed. Even if they weren't afraid of prison, they still had their product seized by the authorities. They could walk free, and still be in a world of trouble, The Colombians didn't care how the product was lost; the person who had it last is responsible. If the cops seized fifty kilos when they arrested you, they weren't giving it back and you're still the guy responsible for those fifty kilos, or their value in cash. Failure to come up with one or the other meant certain death.

Kevin always found that those guys were always the most willing to deal.

As he became more familiar with the process and the people involved, Kevin went undercover.

Even he was shocked by the amounts of cash involved, and how cavalier the participants treated millions of dollars. At first, he investigated small-time dealers or those associated with the Italian Mafia. That was a huge disappointment for Kevin. His war was with the Colombian traffickers, not those they were supplying. But after a string of successes, the DEA aimed him at the Colombians and lit his fuse.

In his undercover role, Kevin posed as a shady bank manager named Kevin Edwards. He would receive a call telling him where he could find a bundle of cash, and then wire-transfer it to several different bank accounts. For his efforts, he would be able to keep a small but significant amount—usually five or six percent, depending on the customer. They were breaking the law, but had been granted an exemption by the attorney general.

Kevin found the irony that traffickers were paying him to launder their money—which gave him evidence the evidence necessary to put them away—and were paying him huge sums that were actually bankrolling the very investigation against them quite satisfying. "Basically, the drug dealers were paying for the investigation we were doing," he said. "So, it's a pretty cool deal." The money went to phones, travel, car rentals, and even buildings. But, to Kevin's dismay, not to pay for the overtime agents had logged on the cases.

The transactions themselves were simple. The DEA had a working arrangement with Bank of America. Kevin would get a call from a broker, directing him to travel to New York, Chicago, Houston, Los Angeles, or Atlanta, but mainly New York, sometimes as often as three times a week. He'd be given a code number, like 33, and when he arrived, he'd get a message on his pager that began with the code, and ended with a local phone number. Kevin would then call the number to set up the transaction. "So, I'd call that person and they would say, 'Hey, meet me on 73rd and 3rd tomorrow at 4 p.m. Wear a suit with a red tie and I'm going to hand you a duffle bag.'"

After that, the local cops would be onto the guy. They'd follow him, hoping to find a stash house. "If he's dropping $1 million to us today, he's dropping $1 million to somebody else tomorrow," Kevin said. "And we're hoping there's $5 million to $10 million in that house." More money meant more evidence.

The DEA would also investigate the phone number. "Hopefully, he's paged us to a cell phone; you know, that's your biggest hope," Kevin said. "A lot of times, they'd page to a call-in center some-where, the guys who are that smart. But sometimes, especially if it happens to be a Dominican guy as opposed to a Colombian guy . . . they were not as sophisticated . . . and that individual would nor-mally call us, page us to a cell phone, that was their own cell phone." Having a suspect's cell phone number was an evidence gold mine. "The task force officers up in New York would love that because, within twenty-four hours, they've got a wiretap on that phone," he said. "So, they're hearing everything he's doing after that."

The contact would usually be someone familiar—Kevin had a standing policy of meeting any contact at least once before doing any business with them. It was more an effort to make the other guy feel more confident about the transaction, to know he was giv-ing the cash to the right person.

Another confidence-building tool Kevin used was to make sure he did not appear too eager to make a deal. Cops have unlimited time to make deals and really want to get them done; everybody involved in trafficking knew that. Real bankers don't. So, Kevin made sure his contacts were informed that he put strict time limits on all deals, and was unwilling to cut any other corners, either.

Occasionally, he'd get a contact who would ask if he could wait two or three days for the money. Kevin would refuse. "No, I'm out of here. I'm going back tonight," he'd say. "If we reconstitute this deal, I'll come back tomorrow. I'm going home." The fact that he desperately wanted to get back to Miami didn't hurt either.

It didn't always go to plan, though. Kevin had cultivated an informant from Philadelphia named Russell who had gotten into trouble when he was caught with an amount of heroin that wasn't really that significant, but was big enough to virtually assure a conviction and a minimum five-year sentence. He was desperate to make a deal, but since his suppliers had already been arrested, he didn't have much to bargain with. When he started talking about how he had been involved in money laundering, the DEA sent him to Kevin.

One of their first jobs was in New York. The deal started simply enough, with the contact telling Russell and Kevin to meet him at a Burger King at 4 o'clock. As an identifier, they agreed Kevin should wear a Red Sox cap, because that's not something you see in New York very often.

Four o'clock came and went with Kevin and Russell waiting in the Burger King. After an hour elapsed, Kevin—still playing the impatient banker—told Russell to cancel the deal. "Get on the phone to your people in Colombia," he told him, "and call it off."

Russell did, and returned to the Burger King to talk with Kevin. If he couldn't pull off a simple transaction like this, Kevin told him, he was "off the deal"—that meant he'd have to face a judge and jury.

Just as they were standing up and getting ready to leave the restaurant, a guy burst through the doors. Kevin described him as "sweaty and anxious" and could tell that he had been running for some time. The guy handed Kevin a duffel bag and took off without saying a word.

Kevin and Russell went back to their hotel. The DEA had provided him with a cash-counting machine, and he was putting the contents of the duffel bag—$500,000 in crisp hundred-dollar bills shrink-wrapped in cellophane—when he received a telephone call. It was the New York City cops who had been providing surveillance for the drop.

They told Kevin that they had tailed the man to a pay phone and watched as he started crying mid-call, and then began slamming the receiver against the phone.

That gave Kevin an idea, one that would help Russell. "You have just been given a gift," Kevin told him. "You need to get on a phone right now and retell those people down there in Colombia that you didn't receive the money, the deal was canceled, and you're not responsible."

Russell looked Kevin in the eye. "But, Kevincito," he said. "They'll kill him."

"Yeah, they probably will," Kevin replied. "But you'll be clean as a whistle because he handed the bag to somebody but there's no way that he can prove that he handed it to the right person, because there's plenty of people in that place with a hat on. He never said a word to us, he knew he never said a word to us."

"Kevin, if I make that final phone call like that, they are going to kill him," Russell said. "I just can't do it. I can't do it."

But Kevin insisted, and changed his tack. He told his informant that they didn't know for certain that they'd kill the guy. "But this I know, I can make a phone call and get you a hearing with a judge and you'll pretty much be given probation and won't do any jail time," Kevin told him. He then sweetened the deal by telling Russell that he was eligible for twenty percent of the cash as a reward.

Russell thought about it. If he made the call, he'd skip jail and make a quick $100,000. After much deliberation, he asked Kevin: "Can I have a drink?"

Kevin smiled and took Russell down to the hotel bar. Russell ordered a double-scotch and gulped it down. Then he looked Kevin in the eye, and said: "I'll do it."

Russell made the call, and two days later, Kevin received another call from the New York City cops. They told him that they had tracked the guy down, and set up a surveillance team on his apartment. They watched the door for two days, but he never came out. So, they broke in. The Colombians had gotten there before them, though. The guy was dead. "Executed," Kevin would later say. "Shot in the head."

Years later, Russell was at a party with Kevin. After some small talk, Kevin brought up the deal in New York and told him that the guy had died. He asked his old informant if he thought they were responsible for his death.

"Ah, he deserved it," Russell answered. "My conscience is clear."

He wasn't the only person involved in one of Kevin's operations to be killed. Another informant, this one based in Panama, was desperate to get out of trouble, so he started feeding Kevin information about cocaine being moved by the Colombians through Panamanian freighters. He was an excellent informant, giving not just exact times, dates, and locations, but even providing the serial numbers of individual shipping containers.

After a quick succession of large drug seizures made possible by his information, Kevin told the Panamanian to lay low because he had heard that people were "starting to put two and two together."

The guy agreed, but it was too late. A couple of days later, his wife received a box in the mail. Inside were two severed hands. The Panamanian authorities had to tell her that the fingerprints on the hands matched her husband's.

When Kevin would return to Miami with the cash, he'd really play the part of a banker. "There was a bank we had a special arrangement with," Kevin later said. "The bank counts the money,

puts it in a security vault . . . and [makes] wire transfers to the various accounts." It was an evidence gold mine. He knew who had the
cash, how much, and also who was getting it.

Kevin rarely handled any actual cash, though. Instead, he would
have an informant make the pickup while he and his team recorded
the transaction on video. Guys would hand over backpacks or duffel
bags with between $250,000 and $2 million in cash, and Kevin would
get the whole thing on tape, fly the money to the bank in Miami,
give "his" cut to the DEA, and transfer the rest back to Colombia.

As they began to trust Kevin Edwards, the guys in Colombia
would make specific requests for luxury products instead of money.
Kevin found himself shopping for, buying, and shipping items as
far ranging as Rolexes and refrigerators. But the important guys
usually wanted the same thing—vehicles. It happened so often that
Kevin got used to buying luxury cars and trucks and doing all com-
plicated paperwork necessary to ship them to Colombia legally.
The preferred vehicle at the time was the Toyota Land Cruiser. The
big truck had long since displaced the Land Rover for having the
reputation as the toughest off-roader, but was also very powerful,
durable and by the 1980s, had grown to be quite luxurious as well.
And they were hard to get in Colombia, further cementing them as
a status symbol to be envied.

Traffickers were hardly the only people who wanted Land
Cruisers, though. So, when a Colombian kingpin sent Kevin an
order for ten of them to give to his most trusted men, an idea
emerged in the crafty DEA agent's mind.

Kevin walked into a South Florida Toyota dealership that he
had become very familiar in and plunked down $1 million in
cash that he'd just collected in New York City a few days earlier in
exchange for ten Land Cruisers. He then faxed all the paperwork to
Colombia, and told his contact there that the trucks would be on
the next freighter out of Miami.

They weren't. He had a contact in Colombia that owed him a favor. Kevin convinced him to print up a press release that claimed the ship carrying the cars sank in a freak tropical storm with all of its crew and cargo lost. He sent the fake story to several Colombian media outlets. Many believed it, and the sad story appeared in some of the nation's most prestigious newspapers.

There was little the Colombia drug lord could do but shrug. It certainly couldn't be blamed on his pal, Kevin Edwards, the trust-worthy banker. It was an act of God. Besides, it was only a lousy million bucks anyway.

Still, the fake tragedy allowed the DEA's South Florida office to add ten brand-new Toyota Land Cruisers to its own fleet.

He became an expert at money laundering, and he—or at least Kevin Edwards—developed a reputation as being among the best in the business. Eventually, he was called in to do business in Colombia. Kevin still takes great pride in being able to drop a half-million bucks off in Bogotá, collecting evidence the whole time, with the bad guys none the wiser.

He recalls sitting there in a food court in a shopping mall in downtown Bogotá—after the drop-off was made there and won-dering if Alex ever ate there. Alex, unaware, was not far away, but was not the kind to person to eat at shopping center food courts anymore. The fact that the money Kevin had laundered had been part of an operation Alex was part of wasn't known to either of them until much later.

Kevin had Alex on his mind a few days earlier. The *Miami Herald* had done a feature story on the two of them. Much to Kevin's dis-may, they portrayed his old friend as some kind of dashing swash-buckler type, not the low-life trafficker Kevin considered him.

It wasn't just that Alex had become something of an outlaw celeb-rity that bothered Kevin, it was the fact they were inextricably tied to each other. Kevin and Alex, the childhood friends, the wrestling buddies from *Sports Illustrated*. Now they were on opposite sides of the law, and the media played on that. While he recognized that it was kind of comic in an ironic sort of way, it got pretty old after a while. Now that everybody he knew was making the "Hey, you seen Alex lately?" joke, it had gotten a lot less funny.

In fact, Alex was up to a lot more than Kevin, his friends, the media, or even the DEA knew about at the time.

*   *   *

By the late 1990s, a lot had changed in the cocaine transportation business. Consistent and intense political pressure from the United States had helped reorganize the law of the seas, and had also prompted other countries to step up their drug interdiction efforts. The DEA had received more personnel, technology, and equipment and were more than prepared to use it all.

And it had been working. In 1997, Alex had bought a yacht, the Five Stars, in Venezuela. On its second trip to Florida, it had been seized by the DEA, along with nine hundred kilos of cocaine.

Alex was on the hook for the nine hundred kilos, and he had been wondering exactly how he could get freighter-sized loads to the United States and Europe without having to worry so much about interdiction from law enforcement. It was a problem that occupied his always inquisitive, mechanically adept mind.

He was driving in Bogotá, not far from the shopping center where Kevin made his money drop (and at about the same time), with his new right-hand man, Wayne Dillon, another Floridian—he was from Islamorada, the same town in the Keys that the potheads from Alex's first gang were from—and he, too, was a fugitive from American justice.

When they pulled up beside a tanker truck, something about how much fuel the cylindrical tanker trailer could hold intrigued Alex.

And that's when he had his eureka moment. How about a submarine? They'd been around for ages, so the technology involved couldn't be secret anymore, or even all that hard to understand. If he could build a submarine, he would be able to get tons of coke anywhere he wanted, and the chances of him getting caught appeared to be negligible. Dillon agreed that it was a brilliant plan—if they could pull it off.

Alex put his heart and soul into the plan in a way that even Kevin would have admired if it had been on the other side of the law. First, Alex acquired the plans to a World War II-era German diesel-electric U-boat from a historical society via mail order. Then—through go-betweens—he ordered three rolled steel tubes from the Fruehauf Trailer Corporation in Belgium. Together, they measured more than one hundred feet long.

He then had them trucked to an old warehouse he had rented from another trafficker, a friend named Miguel Guerrero. It was totally nondescript from the outside, tucked off a highway— Carrera 2—just outside of Facatativá, a small, sleepy town up in the mountains north of Bogotá that specializes in cultivating flowers. Guerrero even supplied him with tools and workers, who bunked in a building next door to the factory.

They made a lot of noise and employed a lot of people, but nobody ever dropped a dime on them. After years of the cartels fighting with the government and paramilitary groups, people in towns such as Facatativá knew better than to get inquisitive and start asking questions about work going on in a warehouse without any signs that it was frequently visited by men who drove fancy cars and wore expensive suits and gold watches. As if to drive the point home that the traffickers were in charge of the area, Facatativá was home to a prison that was reserved for police officers who had given into temptation, sided with the cartels, and had gotten caught.

After about three years, Alex and Dillon had a boat. At more than a hundred feet long and weighed in at over a hundred tons, it was the biggest submarine ever to be built for non-government purposes, and it was designed to be capable of diving three hundred feet under the surface.

If it worked, it would change the face of drug trafficking forever.

Alex had built up an enviable number of contacts all over Colombia, and he put out word that he needed someone to help him with a seagoing vessel. The guy who supplied airplanes to his friends told him that he knew a Ukrainian who had two friends in Colombia who had been in the Soviet Navy—submariners, he thought.

Alex couldn't believe his luck. After some introductions, Alex turned on the charm and started sending cash to the sailors' families back in Moscow as a show of good faith.

Eventually, they showed up at the Facatativá facility. After an initial tour of the boat and consultation with their own plans, they told Alex and Dillon that the motor and hull were basically fine, but they had to tear out all the aluminum pieces Alex had used to save weight—it messes with the onboard batteries, they told him—and to redesign the ballast tanks, outlets, and pumps as well as the fuel lines. They also fitted it with a decompression chamber, so that its pilot and crew would not suffer from the bends if he had to surface or dive quickly.

Once finished, the sub—which they had dubbed the Twinkie—was to be cut into three pieces and loaded on trucks to be taken to Barranquilla, where it would be reassembled and launched off Colombia's north coast. The plan was to ship 10,000 kilos to Spain, where the price of cocaine was still very high, and where Alex had cultivated many contacts, primarily British. The risks were high—the round-trip was not too far from 10,000 miles—but the rewards were astronomical. Each successful mission would be worth nearly a third of a billion dollars.

Just before the planned trip to Barranquilla, Dillon had been out partying with an old friend, a fellow trafficker. Dillon drunkenly told his pal that there was something he just had to see, so they jumped in Dillon's car and drove to the factory in Facatativá. The guards, recognizing Dillon, let them in.

His old friend was amazed by the submarine, and told Dillon that it was a brilliant idea. Then they headed back into Bogotá to continue partying.

A few days later, Dillion's friend was arrested and held for questioning. Facing extradition to the US and a long prison sentence, he remembered what he had seen and told his interrogators that he could give up something far bigger than his operation in exchange for leniency.

Hours later, the chief of the DEA's Bogotá office, Leo Arreguin, received a call from General Luis Ernesto Gilibert Vargas, chief of the national police and grandson of the force's founder. Gilibert asked Arreguin if he'd like to go on a helicopter ride with him, giving no other details. Certain it would be worth his while, Arreguin agreed to go.

Landing in Facatativá, Arreguin quickly (and correctly) assessed it to be a poor, agrarian region. But he did notice that one building, the one Gilibert was leading him to, had a number of state-of-the-art video security cameras attached to it.

"We thought it was going to be some kind of laboratory," he later recalled. "But then I saw the submarine—it was the biggest thing I ever saw." He later admitted that the DEA had nowhere near the capability needed to detect such a craft in the open ocean, and wasn't even sure that the Coast Guard or even the navy would have been able to spot it without being tipped off ahead of time.

When he found out about the submarine, Kevin immediately and correctly assumed it was Alex's simply because he had never met another trafficker that was nearly as smart as his old friend, or as bold. He only wished Alex had used his powers for good instead of trafficking cocaine.

Alex was at home watching TV when he found out about the seizure. The news of the submarine's discovery was the lead story on every news channel. As Colombian police and military, along with DEA agents, swarmed the factory, they were joined by the international media, who angled every story on how shockingly audacious the Colombian traffickers had become.

They marveled at how technically advanced and comfortable the submarine was a—a man could stand up inside without having to worry about ducking on his way through doors.

It was a submarine, but it was hours away from the nearest coast. They were clearly impressed, not only at the machine itself, but the massive undertaking it would take to move it from Facatativá all the way to Barranquilla, its logical destination.

Since submarine design plans with Cyrillic text were found at the site (left behind by Alex's Muscovite friends), many media sources speculated that the Russian Mafia was responsible.

But Alex wasn't feeling good about his accomplishment. He was out $5 million in expenses and three years' work. Still, he felt buoyed by the fact that the authorities and media all agreed that the sub was not only impressive, but in all likelihood, seaworthy. BBC News even quoted Gilibert as saying: "The technology is advanced and the workmanship of high quality."

Alex rededicated himself to the idea of building another submarine, but on a much smaller scale and with a far smaller budget. In fact, what he was putting together in a rented warehouse in downtown Medellín was what the DEA calls a "semi-submersible"—a craft that is mostly under the water's surface, but does not have the capability to dive.

After three months, Alex and Dillon had the craft trucked through a rain forest to a then-isolated beach on the north coast called Palomino. Alex had paid off a heavily armed anti-government rebel group to provide protection while they assembled the sub on the sand in the darkness overnight.

When they finished, Dillon volunteered to captain the boat on its initial test run. He had been feeling guilty, he told Alex, about messing up the Twinkie project.

With the sun about to rise, the rebels guarding the operation began to become agitated. They didn't like the idea of hanging out with traffickers on a beach in broad daylight. The police could arrive, or—worse yet—the military. They told Alex and his crew to hurry.

And they did. Nobody noticed the damage that the hurried fork-lift driver had done when he moved the sub into the water. And Dillon and the two Colombians on his crew didn't notice that the craft was slowly filling with sea water as it made its way out, at least at first.

When they got about two hundred feet away from shore, the two crewmen saw that the sub was taking on water at an alarming rate. They both dove into the surf and swam for shore.

As Alex and his crew watched in horror, the nose of the sub began to rise until it was pointed straight up at the early morning sky. Then the sub slipped straight down, taking Dillon to the bottom. Neither was ever seen again.

Alex was out of the submarine business.

CHAPTER 14

"Kevin Says Hello"

Although Kevin had developed a sterling reputation with the DEA, even he was not above suspicion. He was in the office in Doral when his supervisor asked him to come into a conference room. He was seated with twelve other agents he had worked with when an FBI officer began to read them their Miranda rights.

Shocked and surprised—and totally unaware of what he was being accused of—Kevin refused to answer any questions. "I've been an agent long enough, so I said, you know, that's all fine and well, but if you're going to read me my Miranda warnings, I'm not talking to you," he recalled, "I have an attorney, he's over there, go talk to him. I'm not talking to anybody under Miranda."

That made the FBI agent more suspicious. The other DEA guys all talked. What, if anything, he thought, was Kevin hiding?

The truth was that he wasn't hiding anything. He was just protecting himself.

He would learn that the investigation he was working on in Panama overlapped with one that the CIA had launched, and involved many of the same people. He recalled being in the middle of an investigation in Tegucigalpa—the capital of Honduras—when a squad of CIA agents told him and his men to leave immediately and not ask any questions. Kevin figured that there was some big player in Honduras that was moving a lot of drugs, but the CIA had their own reasons to make sure he didn't go to prison.

One of the DEA agents involved had been found to be taking bribes from a suspect in Panama. When the suspect was interviewed about other agents he had worked with, he rattled off a long list that included Kevin's name.

But the truth was that the guy had never worked with Kevin, had never even met him. It was simply a case of a scared suspect attempting to give as much information after his arrest—not all of it valuable or even true. Everyone in the cocaine business knew Kevin's name by then, and the guy had simply made it as part of a list of agents he hoped he could accuse. Perhaps it was an honest mistake. The bribes, he said, were that he had procured the services of prostitutes for the agents on his list.

That could hardly have outraged Kevin more. Nothing could be farther from his character than to accept sex from a prostitute in exchange for hiding sensitive information.

He was investigated by the DEA's internal affairs as well as the Department of Justice's Office of Professional Responsibility. They also discovered travel vouchers in his name that had been used for personal trips.

Of course, they found nothing amiss with Kevin. Indeed, Kevin proved that he had never been in contact with his accuser in Panama and that the signatures on the misused travel vouchers might have said "Kevin Pedersen" but they did not match his signature at all.

Several agents were in trouble, including Kevin's direct supervisor (who he actually had to testify against), and—after an in-house suspension of nearly eighteen months—Kevin was given an official

DEA letter of clearance. Through it all, Kevin stayed positive. "I knew I had been through worse," he said.

But the media only reported the accusations, not the vindication. Kevin felt like his reputation as an agent had been tarnished by an irresponsible informant and by a fellow agent who smeared his good name for a few lousy plane rides by forging his signature.

As an apology, the DEA gave him a couple of extra days of paid vacation.

Kevin's role transitioned. He started doing less and less field work and more teaching, which suited him. By then, he had seized, by his own recollection, "upwards of" $100 million in cash and "put hundreds of people in jail," so he had some expertise to pass on.

* * *

Back in Medellín, Alex found himself in an unfamiliar situation. He was out of money. Not only had the submarine plans cost him millions, he had devoted so much time and effort to it that he had not been working.

But there was always product to be moved, and he knew that all he had to do was wait, and business would come to him.

It didn't take long. Just a couple of days after he returned from Barranquilla, Alex's phone rang. It was an old friend, a trafficker, from Cali. He told Alex that a friend of his had a big load he needed to get into Florida.

Alex agreed to take on the operation, and the two arranged to meet at a popular Pastelería Santa Elena dessert restaurant in the El Poblado neighborhood of downtown Medellín, which was populated mainly by wealthy foreigners. Alex asked his old friend for a favor—he needed $40,000 to take care of some immediate expenses. The friend agreed, saying it would be no problem.

Alex drove to El Poblado in his least conspicuous vehicle—a

brand-new, bright white Jeep Wrangler TJ. The friend was already
at the restaurant. They had a pleasant conversation, arranged the
pickup and drop, and the friend handed over $40,000 in an enve-
lope. It was, as Alex had been assured, no problem.

Alex got back in his Jeep feeling good. He was beginning to get
back in the game, to start shaking off the submarine debacle and
make money the way he always had.

As he got on Avenida Bolivariana—an elevated highway that is
the quickest way in and out of downtown Medellín—he was dismayed at the slow traffic. He was being waved over. It was a police
roadblock.

Alex didn't think much of it. They happened all the time. The
cops would stop everybody, ask them a few questions, look at their
identification then let them go. Alex wondered if there was anyone
stupid enough to get caught that way. More likely, he thought, it
was just a great way for police to look busy and maybe collect a bribe
or two. He had identification that he'd used tons of times without
a problem. And if some cop gave him trouble, Alex thought to
himself, he'd just peel a couple of hundreds off his stack of cash and
it would all be over and he'd be back on his way.

Alex slowed the Jeep down and pulled over. He did not think
anything of the fact that there were so many cops, and that some of
them were outfitted in full SWAT gear.

Cops swarmed around the Jeep, getting Alex to pop the hood and
open the rear cargo door. They were clearly looking for something.
As they searched, an older, clearly high-ranking plainclothes officer
approached the driver's side window. Politely, Alex lowered the
window, and was reaching into his back pocket to get his driver's
license—which identified him as Francisco Cruz—when the cop
waved at him to stop.

"That won't be necessary," he said. "I don't need to see your
driver's license, Alex."

A chill shot through Alex's arteries. Alex. Not Francisco or Juan or even Alejandro. The cop—who was actually an Interpol agent—called him Alex. It was a name he had not heard since he had fled from Florida all those years ago.

Alex looked over at the cop. Smiling, the senior officer turned the clipboard he was carrying to show Alex. It was the picture of him that ran in the newspaper from the 1976 Florida state wrestling championship. Alex was looking at a young, smiling version of himself—full of hopes and dreams—wearing his Panthers wrestling singlet with pride and purpose.

It was over. Alex's high-flying days as a trafficker were done. The friend he had just met in the bakery was working as an undercover agent to stay out of prison, and the whole Cali operation had been a set-up.

The Colombians were proud that they caught the big fish. In the official media release they issued after his arrest, the quoted a senior national police official as saying: "DeCubas was certainly as important as Pablo Escobar, the former head of the Medellín Cartel, for the enormous quantities of cocaine shipped abroad from Colombia." While that certainly was an exaggeration (at his peak, Escobar made $420 million a week, and once used $2 million in cash to fuel a bonfire), DeCubas had been a significant player.

A few hours after the arrest, Kevin Curtis overheard another DEA agent in the Bogotá office say that a trafficker named Alex DeCubas had been picked up in El Poblado. Curtis was stunned. Had they really arrested Alex? He asked the agent to make sure it was Alex DeCubas, born in Cuba and raised in Miami. The agent checked with his contacts in Medellín. It was indeed the same Alex DeCubas who had wrestled for Palmetto High.

Curtis got on the phone with his own people to find out the details. They were taking Alex to be processed at a secure facility in Bogotá. The Colombian agent asked Curtis if he wanted to come down and see him. Of course he did. "I'll be there in twenty," he replied, and grabbed his jacket.

As is traditional, the authorities let Alex stew in an interrogation room for a while. Curtis was escorted into the interrogation room by a US marshal. He later said that, although Alex looked calm, even relieved, Curtis could tell that the life of a fugitive had been rough on him. He had heard people say that Alex had undergone several plastic surgeries to alter his appearance, but he looked just like Curtis thought he would, maybe a bit flabbier and more haggard, but definitely the same guy in the picture.

After introductions, Curtis didn't question Alex. Instead, he told him about the pending charges and what was going to happen to him over the next few days as the extradition process played out. When it had finished, Curtis told Alex he would be flown to Miami to face trial.

After Alex told him he understood, they were just about done. "Just one more thing," Curtis said. "Kevin says hello."

Alex didn't say anything, but he did tear up.

*   *   *

Danny, Alex's son, was shocked when he heard the news that his father had been arrested and was being taken away to America. Not only did the eight-year-old have to deal with suddenly being fatherless, but everything he had been told, everything he knew, was a lie.

The man he knew as his dad—the upstanding engineer Juan Vasquez—was actually a Cuban-American drug smuggler named Alex DeCubas.

People started talking. The neighbors, his schoolmates, even his teachers. Danny was scared. His mother knew it wasn't safe for them in Medellín anymore. She and Danny moved to Bogotá, where nobody knew them, to start a new life.

* * *

After a few days, the extradition process went by without inci-
dent. Curtis and two US marshals took Alex to Bogotá's El Dorado
International Airport, and took their seats in the last row of a
United Airlines' direct flight to Miami.

"He was absolutely non-confrontational," Curtis later recalled.
"Polite, a perfect gentleman." In fact, Curtis later admitted that
they got along quite well—"something clicked"—and decided that
Alex was "just a nice guy who did some bad things."

That was often the case. Alex got along with most of the law
enforcement officers whose job it was to take away his freedom. He
did, however, complain that one of the US Marshals, Joe Godsk,
had asked him, "How's Tiny?" That was not only a reference to his
son, Danny—Alex felt that innocent kids should be left out of their
business—and he said he found it unprofessional for the investiga-
tors to share such personal information with someone not directly
related to his case.

That feeling of camaraderie would later become a commonplace reaction to Alex. Cops, agents, correctional staff, and even
prosecutors would fall for his charm, and wish him well. There
was a notable holdout, though. James Burke, head of the No Mas
Task force, said he noticed that even veteran DEA agents who had
devoted their lives to stopping traffickers were palling around with
Alex, like he was one of their own. He told me that he thought it
was unprofessional.

He and Pelletier were waiting at the airport in Miami for Alex
and Curtis to arrive. Burke was curious to see Alex because he, too,
had heard that he had altered his appearance in Colombia to avoid
capture. "The first thing I noticed was his hair plugs," he later told
me. "They looked like they still needed work."

They interviewed him. Alex wouldn't talk much at first, and

certainly gave every indication that he was not about to give anyone else up. He did, however, talk openly about his submarine projects. He expressed sadness, but no guilt, over how Dillon had died in the second one, and nothing but pride in the size and scope of the first one. "Didn't you see the pictures?" he asked Pelletier.

* * *

Once news that Alex was back in South Florida, this time as a prisoner, emotions raged. Alex waved to his tearful mother Nena—who still refuses to believe her son had anything to do with drugs—and told Godsk that he was worried about what would happen to Danny in Colombia.

Most of his old friends were happy to see that Alex was still alive, but were, as a group, deeply disheartened over the circumstances of his return to South Florida. "I'm very sad to see that after fifteen years, he's coming back now shackled and is looking at a very, very grave situation given the allegations against him," William Jones, a friend of Alex's from the Palmetto football team who later became a Miami attorney. "People just never have let him die out of their mind—he was that good of an athlete; he was that powerful a character."

* * *

Kevin was waiting in the courtroom. It felt strange for him to be a spectator and not a participant after all the court time he had logged in his years as a DEA agent. It was just before Christmas 2004, and, although he was almost overwhelmingly busy, Kevin would not have missed this for anything. He had to see Alex, alive and in captivity, for himself.

Word that Alex had been caught spread through Miami quickly. Andrew DeWitt, a former teammate of Alex's who got him his job at the tool store, said that it was all anybody in their little set of friends could talk about.

Even Kevin. And, more than anybody else, Kevin was relieved that Alex was arrested. "I was sure they were going to call and tell me he was dead," he told me. He later said, "I was very surprised that he was arrested and that he actually showed up in the United States."

Kevin didn't know what he was going to see when Alex finally arrived. He hadn't seen his old pal, his protector, in twenty-four years. While he had joined the DEA in hopes to fight the war on drugs, Alex—friend or not—was a general in the opposing army, flooding South Florida with the same substance that had taken away his command in the army and his wife.

He had every right to hate Alex, but he just couldn't. Many people use their religion as window dressing or even a false front for other agendas, but not Kevin Pedersen. He was as sincere in his Christian beliefs as he was in everything else. He knew that the cornerstone of Christian theology was redemption through forgiveness. Alex might have been his adversary, even his enemy, in the War on Drugs, but that was done now. Alex had been caught and was set to pay a reasonable penalty for what he had done. What Alex needed was to be forgiven and to be allowed to move on with his life.

Alex was led into the courtroom wearing an orange jumpsuit, handcuffs and leg shackles. Kevin could see that he had lost some hair and added some lines to his face and some padding to his belly, but he was still the same old charming Alex. "The funny thing is," Kevin told me. "He looked smaller than I remembered."

When the two men locked eyes, Alex grinned and waved at his old pal. *Same old Alex*, Kevin thought. But then he thought about the situation seriously, and realized that this was not the same old Alex, and it gave him hope. Kevin believed that the only way Alex could move on with his life, away from the drugs and crime would be if he had been humbled. It was the only way, Kevin believed, for Alex to make the break he needed. He was relieved to see what he interpreted as genuine remorse in his old friend's eyes before he looked down. "The Alex of old" he later said, "would have stared me down."

They hadn't seen each other since the night Kevin walked into the Crown Lounge in 1980. So much had happened to both of them since then.

Kevin had heard some wild tales about Alex's exploits in Colombia, and believed most of it. The evidence given at the trial he attended told him only a tiny slice of what he already knew.

Kevin said that he wasn't happy about Alex's arrest the way he had been with many other traffickers; it wasn't a "we got him" moment. He felt good, he said, that such a major trafficker had been put out of business, and he was relieved that Alex was not going to come back to the United States in a body bag. But he also felt sad, he said, that it had all unfolded the way it had. Alex, with all his abilities, his strength, his mechanical skills, and his charm, had wasted all his tremendous potential because of the lure of easy drug money. He could have been just about anything, and been good at it—an architect, a teacher, a salesman, even a politician. And now he was looking to spend what would probably amount to the rest of his life behind bars. "I did not rejoice," he said.

Facing overwhelming evidence against him, Alex pleaded guilty to trafficking twenty-four tons of cocaine into the United States. Although that number is probably nowhere near the total amount many believe that he actually moved, it still represents anywhere from $250 million to $1 billion in wholesale value, depending on the variations in market prices.

Prior to sentencing, his lawyer sought character witnesses among Alex's old friends and associates. One of them was Kevin, who was surprised when he was served with a subpoena. Dutifully, Kevin reported to the defense attorney, but warned him: "Be very careful what you're asking me to do here." He was not called to the stand.

Neither did Alex speak on his own behalf. But plenty of others did. Alex received glowing reports of his character from dozens of well-wishers. Even correctional officers and police reported that he was easy to get along with, charming, and spent his time reading books and "trying to better himself."

Pelletier tempered their glowing reports, though. "It's obvious when this defendant puts his mind to something, he's very good at it," he said. "Unfortunately, he put his mind to drug trafficking."

Still, the judge's hands were tied by sentencing guidelines and minimums. Twenty-four tons of cocaine (not to mention the tons of marijuana and thousands of Quaalude tablets he'd moved) was just too much to allow for leniency. US District Judge Joan Lenard could have given him a life sentence, but instead chose to put Alex behind bars for thirty years. He would get out when he was seventy-six years old.

CHAPTER 15

Full Circle

Thirty years is a long time, and seventy-six years old makes you an old man, no matter who you are. Alex knew he wanted nothing less than to spend the next three decades in prison. So, he decided to talk. It's not like he was the only guilty one, he said to himself, why should he have to take the fall for everyone?

It would have probably helped him more if he had cooperated before his sentencing, but he could still salvage what was left of his life.

So, he talked. And he talked, and he talked. Alex talked about anyone and everyone. In fact, he was in and out of Wilkie D. Ferguson Jr. Federal Courthouse so often, that he was transferred from Federal Corrections Complex Coleman, north of Orlando, to spend almost his entire time behind bars at the Federal Detention Center, which is designed to house pre-trial prisoners only. But it was so close to the courthouse (literally across the street) and Alex was in there pretty well every day, they made an exception for him. Even behind bars, Alex was still special.

The first person he spoke about was the notorious Brian "the

Milkman" Wright, who had been his contact in England. A largely illiterate Irish immigrant who left school at eleven to become a croupier in illegal casinos, Wright admitted to a newspaper reporter that he had never paid a penny in taxes in his life, despite a lifestyle of obvious and ostentatious wealth. He had long been sought by several British police forces who had thus far failed to produce much useful evidence against the slippery gangster. Wright once bet a customs officer a million pounds to one that he'd never get caught. Wright was widely reputed to have bribed jockeys and drugged horses to fix races, as well as flooding London with cocaine.

But, with Alex's help, a British court managed to put Wright away for thirty years.

In a dramatic representation of how many people were telling on who, Colombian kingpin Hernan "El Gordo" (Fatso) Prada had agreed to testify against another old associate when Alex and another trafficker, Mario Astaiza, were testifying against him. Prada admitted to importing tons of cocaine into South Florida, and to have preferred champagne out of gold goblets, but claimed he had quit the cocaine businesses before the statute of limitation-set date that would have made him legally culpable had passed. It was his word against that of Alex and Astaiza, and the jury ruled in his favor.

It was on one of those near-daily courthouse trips that Kevin ran into him again. "The next time I saw him was outside a grand jury room in Miami. Usually, when you're waiting outside that room, it is to testify. No one is allowed inside there except the testifiers," he recalled. "We shook hands, talked, and told him I liked his hair plugs. He was proud of them, I thought they were terrible."

That seemed to normalize things a little between the two, and they began to exchange letters after that. Alex initiated it. His letters were neatly printed on white or yellow lined paper with good grammar and almost no spelling mistakes. They have a friendly, sometimes a little bit self-effacing tone, and are liberally peppered with jokes, after which Alex often wrote "HA-HA-HA" in parentheses. In the letters, he expressed concern for others—Coach Zimbler, who had lost a significant amount of property during Hurricane Katrina, Kevin's son Danny who was serving in Iraq, and his own Danny—and a desire to better himself by taking classes and reading. He told him about some information that he'd learn about other traffickers who he'd met in prison, gave him the name of an "honest marine mechanic" (which he considered a true rarity) to help Kevin with his boat and even gave him his favorite recipe for mahi-mahi.

Kevin didn't answer at first, but once he did, Alex's letters got longer, more personal, and it was obvious he was delighted to hear from his old friend. The first few he closed with "best wishes, Alex," but changed that to "big hugs" later on.

After a little more than nine years, when he was out of useful information and the authorities felt that he had been punished enough, he was released. Alex was a free man.

*   *   *

While Alex was in prison, things did not go well for Danny, Alex's son. He didn't get along with his mother's new husband in Bogotá, and after years of them fighting, she let him go where he wanted. Danny thought life would be better with his father, and he desperately wanted to move to Miami. He'd been attending bilingual schools for most of his life, and his English was fine.

His uncle Luis Jr. was no help. Danny later told me he had seen him "maybe four or five times" in his whole life, and barely knew the man.

But with his dad still behind bars and Danny too young to take care of himself in a foreign country, his family made a compromise. He moved in with his dad's old pal Scott Sherouse in the Bahamas.

Despite the idyllic setting, it did not go well. Danny and Sherouse had problems right from the start, and never really got along. Danny told me that Sherouse was "abusive," and that he could not wait until his father got out of prison, so he could join him in Miami.

After eighteen months, he got his wish early. Sherouse realized that he could not live in the same house with the boy anymore, so he called Miami to see if he could convince any of his old friends to take him in, even though his father was still in prison.

The first people he called were the Pedersen brothers. Mike, who had retired from the Marines, was shocked that Sherouse would make such a request. Not only had Alex entrusted him with the task of looking after his son, but the two didn't see eye to eye at all. Mike and Sherouse could barely speak without getting into a political argument—sometimes almost coming to blows—and he thought it was hypocritical for him to want the boy to be brought up in a home that was so dedicated to the polar opposite of his own views. Kevin also declined the offer. Finally, Sherouse called another old friend—also a former Palmetto High wrestler—to take the boy in. It was only a matter of months before Alex was released.

Danny DeCubas, who had bounced around and through a total of fifteen schools was able to finally land in a Miami high school where he could prepare for his dream of attending college. Miami was the best, and safest, place for him to pursue his dreams of becoming a successful entrepreneur.

*   *   *

Kevin was busy with his own family and interests, and was eagerly looking forward to the next stage of his life. He retired from the DEA in 2012, after having served twenty-one years. He was one of the most highly decorated agents ever to have served.

It was the fulfillment of one of his childhood ambitions, and it had also satisfied the promises he made to himself and his God after he had nearly taken his own life. But it hadn't been easy. The hours, the travel, the tension, and the fear had taken a toll on his family life. "I think that any wife or spouse of a law enforcement officer or federal agent or any spouse with that kind of career, it can be very trying on the spouse, and my hat goes off to any marriage that can handle the highs and lows that come with it. It's not easy. Kevin was gone a lot," said his second wife, Michele. "One of the cases was such a high-level case that after I gave birth to my daughter, Kevin had to literally pull off the side of the road to answer as he carried three phones with him. I was like . . . really? Kevin tried to juggle it all."

It was not long after he retired that he got a call from Coach Zimbler. He was planning a get-together for all the old wrestlers at his place. Kevin was delighted, until he was told that it would also be a welcome home party for Alex.

There was no party when I was decorated by the DEA, he thought to himself, or when Jeff Cutler passed the bar and become a city councilman and vice-mayor of Pinecrest. Dom Gorie had been on four shuttle missions to space, and there was no party for him. Kevin was actually starting to get angry. All Alex did was break the law for pretty much all of his adult life—what was there to celebrate about that? "I had no desire to be there to start with. I just found the whole situation to be strange," Kevin later said. "If I were to psychoanalyze myself, I'd say, 'Why are we having almost a dinner to honor Alex getting out of jail when the rest of us are slugging it away for years doing all the right things and no one threw a dinner for us?'"

But, as he thought about it, Kevin realized that it made sense. In his faith based on forgiveness and redemption, he knew that it was imperative that he help welcome Alex back into the fold. The lessons of the Parable of the Prodigal Son had not been lost on him.

Alex was getting a party not because he deserved one, but because he needed one. Sure, he had lived the high life while making millions in Florida and Colombia, but what did he have now? Alex was being released after nine long years behind bars with no family, no friends, no money, no job, and no way to put his shattered life back together.

Yes, Gorie had been to space, but that was its own reward, and he had gotten recognition enough among his family, friends and even the media. Cutler had become a well-respected lawyer and politician. And Coach Zimbler himself would later be enshrined in the National Wrestling Hall of Fame after a campaign spearheaded by Cutler and several other of his former wrestlers. Kevin himself had been decorated by the DEA and much celebrated by his own friends and family for his accomplishments.

And he lived well. He had his second wife, Michele, and three kids. His oldest, Danny, followed in his footsteps and went to West Point. Serving with an artillery battery commander and a ground liaison officer for both F-35 fighters and A-10 close support aircraft, he distinguished himself while serving in Iraq and Afghanistan, earning both a Bronze Star and a Purple Heart. Just before his dad retired, he left the military to become an analyst at Booz Allen Hamilton, a management consulting company. Kevin also had two daughters with Michele, Krista, and Lauren. Krista was away in college and Lauren in middle school when Kevin left the DEA.

Compared to the position Alex was in, Kevin was living like a king. He knew that it was his duty as a friend, as a neighbor, and as a man of faith to go to the party and help welcome Alex back into the community.

He was dreading the idea, though, that Alex had not changed, that he would talk about his high-flying days as a trafficker without remorse, or even worse, with pride. Good man of faith or not, that would not sit well with Kevin at all.

When he arrived at Zimbler's house, he made his way into the kitchen through the crowd that had gathered around Alex.

As soon as the big man saw him, he pushed away the other well-wishers and engulfed Kevin in a hug. This time, Kevin returned the embrace.

They talked together for hours. While tacitly agreeing not to touch on the big issues that had kept them adversaries for years, they had a great time catching up and laughing. No laughs were bigger that night than the one that erupted after Kevin took out his DEA badge and had a picture taken of himself arm in arm with Alex.

Headed home that night, Kevin felt good about his time with Alex. It wasn't just that he had a pleasant time with an old friend, or that he had done his duty as a man of faith, but he felt like Alex had really put his outlaw lifestyle behind him.

It did not start off auspiciously. Desperate for money, and without much of a resume, Alex gravitated back towards some of his other old friends. Before long, he was rumored to be working in an untitled capacity at Club Cinema, a notorious nightclub operated by Sam Frontera. Because he was a felon, Frontera was not eligible for a liquor license, so the club was actually owned by a series of shell companies and its official decision-maker was actually Frontera's elderly mother back in Michigan.

Alex also talked to the federal prosecutor about easing the travel restrictions that were among the conditions of his early release. He said he "knew some guys" in the "petroleum business" in Venezuela who had plenty of work for him. The federal prosecutor, not delighted by the idea of letting Alex go back to South America—and fully cognizant that he had always traveled to and from Colombia through buffer countries, including Venezuela—declined his request.

At the time, Kevin said that what he wanted to help Alex with his "heart condition, and by that I mean his spiritual heart, not his physical one."

Danny, Alex's son, had been established in Miami, happy to see the last of Sherouse's place in the Bahamas. He'd been dissolute in both Colombia and the Bahamas—hanging out, getting drunk, hooking up. Life had been tough for him, and was dealing with anger issues and other emotional stresses. He felt as though coming to Miami and reuniting with his dad would straighten that all out.

He was partially right. Coming to Miami did help him. He attended Christopher Columbus Catholic High School—which he described to me as an "awesome school"—and did very well. Not only did he succeed academically (he won a national gold medal for Spanish), but he also proved himself to be quite an athlete. To no one's surprise, he just happened to be very good at wrestling.

But he didn't exactly connect with his old man the way he wanted to, the way he expected to. It wasn't an abusive or even adversarial relationship. It was just more distant than Danny had hoped for. "I think prison did something to him," he told me. "Or maybe he is just one of those people who were never meant to be parents."

Danny would persevere, though. He became involved in some local product distribution businesses through friends and his natural skill as an entrepreneur emerged. After high school, he enrolled in Florida International University's Business Administration program.

Alex distanced himself from Frontera after he had been charged with serving alcohol to minors and serving after hours. The media became interested when links between Club Cinema and Frontera and embattled Deerfield Beach mayor Al Capellini surfaced. It didn't take long for them to make a connection between Frontera and Alex. It would, of course, be unwise for Alex to continue hanging around Club Cinema.

Kevin was dismayed and disappointed, he told me at the time.

He wanted to help his old friend get on the right path, and didn't know how.

One thing he could do, he thought, was to lead by example. Kevin had done well for himself. He had a nice home in Palmetto Bay, a quiet, leafy suburb just southwest of Pinecrest. He drove a Mercedes—just like the guys he chased—and had a powerful boat for fishing. But he had gotten his honestly, earning money not just from the DEA, but also from the two tire stores Michele and he owned. He never took a dime that wasn't his, never broke a rule, never rounded a corner or fudged a fact. To him, it was simple, and he had a hard time figuring out why other people didn't understand that success came from hard work and following the rules, even if you were delivered serious blows by fate.

Those were the lessons he tried to teach the kids he coached as a volunteer at Westminster Christian School in Palmetto Bay. He had entered high school as a scrawny little nobody and left as state champion, proving that nobody should ever count themselves out because they didn't look the part. And he had been on the verge of suicide, alone, broke, and desperate. Years later, he was a decorated law enforcement officer, a financial success with a wonderful wife and three admirable children. That proved that there were no hurdles too big to overcome through hard work and perseverance.

It wasn't long after he retired, that Westminster hired Kevin to be their full-time wrestling head coach. It was like a dream come true. Kevin had become what he always wanted to be, a leader of men. He could use his own life experiences to help the young men of Westminster make the right life choices for themselves, and prevent them from taking the wrong path.

Not surprisingly, he was a success. Not just at helping kids to win on the mat, but to absorb his life lessons as well. But there are always a few who are different. Sure, the underdogs took his story to heart, but there were those other guys, the naturals, the ones to whom everything came easy. Kevin realized that they were actually the guys who were in trouble. Kids who knew hardship growing up develop coping mechanisms to deal with situations that don't go their way. But the kids who had never seen adversity, those were the ones looking for an easy ride, and who flipped out when confronted with a difficult situation.

Those guys just couldn't relate to Kevin, at least not as easily as the others. And that's when he came up with his master plan.

It was March 19, 2015, the first practice of the wrestling season. Kevin was in full form, rallying his troops with the kind of inspirational speech rarely heard outside of the military. He finished it by saying that he had a surprise for the boys.

On cue, the gym door opened, and in walked a big and obviously very strong middle-aged man. He strode with a rare confidence, knowing that every eye was on him, and he very clearly liked it.

The boys were dead silent, mesmerized by the imposing figure standing beside Coach Pedersen. "Guys," Kevin said. "I would like to introduce you to assistant coach Alex DeCubas."

*　　*　　*

During the Warriors' practice sessions, the teenagers appreciated the expertise that volunteer coach DeCubas provided every week, especially the heavyweight grapplers. At the same time, this larger-than-life character, even though he had become a middle-aged guy with hair plugs and a beer belly was spoken about quietly after sunset. Was he for real about coaching? Or, was he simply seeking some type of redemption to assist an effort for an early parole release?

There was an opportunity for the young men to have further discussions about their new volunteer coach during a trip in January 2016, when Kevin and Alex guided the Westminster Christian Warriors into Cape Coral to take on the Mariner High School

Fighting Tritons as part of the Florida West Coast Lely Duals Wrestling Tournament. The Fighting Tritons' coach was none other than Mike Pedersen.

Even though Westminster's heavyweight Anthony Machado and lightweight Jordan Interian scored perfect 5–0 records, the older Pedersen brother won the day, as Mariner High knocked Westminster Christian out of the match and into seventh place. Kevin Pedersen was in good spirits, though, and pointed out that Army beat Navy in football earlier that season, so he didn't feel all that bad about losing to his Annapolis-graduate brother.

Not long after a bout of throat cancer pushed Zimbler to retire to a less demanding administrative position, he had the chance to see his two wrestlers in action as coaches. Zimbler—whose family-style wrestling program produced an astronaut, a marine fighter pilot, a corporate lawyer and politician, a commercial airline pilot, a DEA agent, a cocaine kingpin, and now several wrestling coaches—could hardly have been more pleased.

Zimbler had previously stopped by to see the Warriors practice, but had not yet been to a live match until the 2016 home season opener. The Westminster Christian gym was buzzing with conversations about how Coach Pedersen had revitalized the wrestling program and had bred enthusiasm among the teenagers. Oh, and there's this volunteer assistant coach with a colorful past who is, perhaps, seeking redemption.

One wrestling fan offered this verse from the Bible:

"As far as the east is from the west. So far has he removed our transgressions from us."

—Psalm 103:12

Clearly, that fan believed that everyone deserves a second chance, even if they've been involved with a deadly drug that plagued their very own Pinecrest neighborhoods, not to mention just a few miles from the Dadeland Mall, where the 1979 massacre took place and will be forever remembered as a turning point in the War on Drugs. Another fan in the stands responded, "Hope so, and we'll see."

While the first home match was supposed to be a reunion with Zimbler, Pedersen, and DeCubas, a gym full of fans couldn't help but wonder about another somewhat odd-looking man who was wearing a baseball cap backwards and trying to look like a thug. He suddenly appeared behind the Warriors bench to take advantage of photo ops. While the kids didn't recognize him, the coaches sure did. It was Scott Sherhouse, who couldn't look more out of place if he tried.

While Alex was making every effort to atone for his sins, he had a hard time distancing himself from the same people—Sam Frontera, Felix Chativa and, of course, Scott Sherhouse—who were at least partially responsible for his path to Westminster from dealer to kingpin to fugitive to convict. What was supposed to be one of the highlights of Kevin Pedersen's coaching career quickly turned into being a major disappointment when he saw DeCubas with Sherhouse. Coach Pedersen realized he would have to deal with those two later, away from the impressionable eyes and ears in the Warriors gym.

The next day, Pedersen was able to focus his energies on the upcoming District State Tournament to be held in the Florida Keys. Feeling confident that his wrestlers were prepared for one of the school's best results in years, he still needed to make sure the young men would reach their potential. Heavyweight Dylan Charlton, in his senior year, had progressed the most, partially due to the extra coaching he had received from DeCubas. As a team captain, he was determined to provide the Warriors with a banner tournament. Machado cheered on his teammates and was one of seven Warriors to advance to the Regionals in Fort Lauderdale. It was the greatest success the school had achieved in many years.

Charlton acknowledged to teammates that even he was surprised at how much he had improved during his final year, which certainly was one filled with unique experiences. After all, how many high school wrestlers could imagine wrestling for a former cocaine kingpin?

Charlton's biggest victories, though, were being named the school's Student of the Year and being selected to attend West Point, coach Pedersen's alma mater. During the Warriors' 2017 season, team captain Machado won a district title, finished third in the regionals to advance to the state tournament, and also earned the distinction of being selected to West Point, where he'd be reunited with Charlton.

"I spoke with one of the assistant wrestling coaches [at West Point]," said Pedersen. "They never heard of back-to-back captains of a team attending West Point."

*   *   *

Almost forty-five years after they met each other on that Suniland Park baseball diamond, and just about thirty-nine years after they were both state wrestling champions and appeared in *Sports Illustrated* together, Kevin Pedersen and Alex DeCubas had gone full circle.

While they had spent most of their adult lives on opposite sides of the War on Drugs, in 2015 they were back where they started, back where they belonged. "I would have loved to be able to change things because I lost the most precious years of my son's life and I can never get that back, if I only knew what I know now," Alex said. "I lost twenty-three years of being able to be a father to my son. I spent thirteen years as fugitive in Colombia, and ten years in prison. No money can ever repay that. Those years are gone."

But being with Kevin and the supportive people at Westminster was probably the best way for him to put that behind him. "That was the perfect place for Alex to come," Kevin later said. "There's a lot of . . . people there who understand forgiveness."

They were no longer soldiers in a war. They were friends again.

The kids on the Westminster wrestling team saw the situation for what it really was. Alex was a big, strong guy with a penchant for showmanship and flair, while Kevin was the little guy who tried really hard and never gave up.

They were just a couple of middle-aged guys in suburban Miami, tossing each other around on the wrestling mat—exactly what they both always intended to be.

Epilogue

For Americans, the very concept of war has changed. For much of our history, one nation fought against another until there was a clear and decisive victory. But that's not what happens anymore. In recent years, it was not the United States against Afghanistan or Iraq, it was the United States against radical Islam fundamentalist elements in those countries and others, including here at home. We don't fight against other countries anymore, we fight against concepts.

One of those concepts, of course, has long been illegal drug importation. On May 13, 2009—almost thirty-eight years after it was declared by President Richard Nixon—Gil Kerlikowske, President Barack Obama's Director of the Office of National Drug Control Policy quietly retired the official name "War on Drugs." Kerlikowske said that there would be no change in the administration's drug trafficking interdiction policy, but he and his advisors had decided that the phrase *War on Drugs* was just too bellicose. Its blatant aggressiveness hinted at severe and outdated concepts such as zero tolerance and sentencing people like marijuana users as though they were violent criminals.

The times have changed, and so has many people's opinions on drugs. Marijuana, once called "Public Enemy Number One" by Nixon, is now legal for recreational use in eight American states and Canada, and only three states still have not decriminalized recreational marijuana use. That would have been unthinkable just a generation ago.

But weed was never really the big problem. Sure, there was some crime associated with trafficking it, but nothing frightening, certainly not all-out war like some parts of the country saw in the 1980s and 1990s. The real culprit, we now know, was cocaine, particularly after crack—the cheap, smokable and intensely addictive form of the drug—appeared, that the violent crime rates exploded in the United States.

It wasn't just Miami; a great portion of America became a war zone as gangs fought over the right to sell on city streets, and law enforcement did their best to put them all out of business.

It was terrifyingly violent, especially for the main participants. Pablo Escobar was shot, barefoot and running for his life, by cops. He had already tortured and killed Fernando Galeano. Jorge Gnecco was hunted down by a group of paramilitary vigilantes.

While none of the major characters in this story were killed (except for Wayne Dillon, who drowned in Alex's second submarine), almost all of them have had guns pointed at them, and Scott Sherouse, Félix Chitiva, David Lemieux, and many others spent long stretches behind bars. Of course, Alex himself spent almost ten years in prison and was also kidnapped twice.

But that's all in the past now. Alex is out and coaching with Kevin, as he should be. And, as they walk the streets of South Florida, no longer do they have to worry about random violence, no longer see the ravages that cocaine and crack had once brought to their very neighborhoods.

Cocaine, and even crack, are still around, of course, but they don't have even a fraction of the users or effect on our lives as they used to. And the gang violence that surrounded it has all but vanished in many places, especially big cities. Take New York for example. Aside from Miami, it was the hardest hit of all American cities by what is known as the crack epidemic. Long portrayed (often unfairly) by movies and TV as a dangerous place, New York succumbed to almost unbelievable levels of violence in the late '80s and early '90s. In 1990, at the peak of crack's hold on its population, the five boroughs recorded an almost incomprehensible 2,262 homicides—that's more than six dead bodies in one American city every day. Alex's cocaine pipeline extended to that city, and Kevin investigated money laundering there. They were both part of the war for New York's streets.

And then it all essentially vanished. As cocaine use in big American cities dwindled, crime rates dropped precipitously. In 2016, there were just 335 homicides in New York City, a drop of more than 85 percent when compared to 1990. Similar crashes have been seen in the rates of robbery (a fall from 100,280 to 15,500 over the same period) and burglary (122,055 to 12,990), both of which are frequently associated with the drug trade. Rates for crimes generally not associated with the drug trade, such as rape and simple assault, have also fallen, but nowhere near as much. New York City, traditionally the world's portal to America, went from a crack-crazed war zone to one of the safest major cities in the world in just a few years.

Even South Florida has calmed down, with Miami-Dade police reporting just 85 homicides in 2015.

There are several theories as to why. One adopted by many, including Kevin, is that law enforcement got better at their job as restrictions on their abilities were lifted and technology improved.

There is some truth to that, of course, but I believe it's a secondary factor, well behind the fact that Americans have been educated about cocaine and its effects. And I don't mean educated by those frequently corny and sometimes ridiculous anti-drug public service announcements that the last couple of generations have been force-fed.

When cocaine rose to popularity in the 1970s, it was because it was cool. It was the recreational drug of choice for movie stars, rock stars, and famous athletes. Having cocaine at your party meant that you had arrived, you were a success, and were someone to be taken seriously. Cocaine was associated with fancy cars, speedboats, Armani, Rolexes, beautiful people, and the high life.

The crack epidemic quickly changed that. The tide turned because we all saw the victims. If not the dead bodies themselves, we all witnessed as the wasted, desperate souls who filled our streets, would steal, beg or sell their bodies for that tiny bit of cash that would get them another hit of crack. To most people, being a crackhead looked pretty much like the worst thing you could be.

Suddenly, next to nobody in the big cities wanted cocaine anymore. It wasn't cool, it wasn't chic, it was—to be perfectly frank—disgusting. Cocaine's popularity might have risen to prominence by what Americans saw in movies and TV, but it essentially died at the sight of the real-life crackhead.

After the poor taste that crack left in our cities' collective mouth soured their taste for cocaine in general, things started looking up. Crime fell off, property values soared, and increased tax revenues improved schools and other essential services—at least in the big cities. Crack—as well as its equally addictive and destructive partner, methamphetamine—moved out of the big cities, for the most part. While New York, Los Angeles, and Miami—the cities hardest hit by the crack epidemic—have essentially put the bulk of cocaine-related violence behind them, smaller cities, suburbs, and even rural areas have not caught on as quickly. Formerly placid communities such as St. Louis, Kansas City, and Cincinnati have now become much more violent than places like New York, Miami, and Los Angeles.

Florida is now actually around the middle of the fifty states when it comes to cocaine use now. But it still serves as a major gateway for cocaine and methamphetamine entry to the United States. Interestingly, combined Colombian and United States efforts have largely smashed the cartels in that nation. While most cocaine is still processed in Colombia, the big-time traffickers and cartels are all now headquartered essentially in Mexico. Law enforcement efforts there—rampant with corruption and fear and far less willing to accept American help like the Colombians did—have been largely ineffective at stopping them. Since it began in earnest, the low-intensity civil war between the cartels and Mexico's military and law enforcement has claimed almost 200,000 lives, and continues to rage. Some spillover violence has affected California, New Mexico, Texas, and especially Arizona, and many have called for stiffer interdiction efforts at the Mexico-US border.

But the Mexican cartels are increasingly growing dependent on domestic and international sales as American taste for cocaine and methamphetamine wanes. According to the US government's Substance Abuse and Mental Health Services Administration, by 2011, the states with the highest rates of cocaine use were Colorado, Vermont, and Rhode Island with Oregon and New Hampshire not far behind. And even they each top out at about one in thirty-two adults having used cocaine at least one time in the past year. The same organization estimates that about one in two hundred Americans have used cocaine in the previous year, and that the proportion continues to drop.

Cocaine and methamphetamine use will probably become even rarer in those places as the images and fates of crackheads and methheads fills the consciousness of their communities. Epidemic drug use tends to end when the results are there to be seen.

That's exactly why the new drug problem that is plaguing many Americans will be much harder to make go away. When cocaine use ceased to be cool, it began to disappear as a problem. But people don't take prescription painkillers—mostly opioids in the same family as heroin and morphine—to be cool or sexy. They take them to feel better.

Opioids were traditionally—and still are—prescribed by physicians to treat chronic pain. They were frequently administered to people with the sorts of professions that led to bad backs and aching knees after decades. Typical users were typically older and had usually earned their aches and pains by years of coal mining in West Virginia, agricultural work in New Mexico, forestry in Washington State, or working on an assembly line in Ohio.

But things have changed. Most of those jobs have been lost to automation or cheap overseas labor. But the opioids have stayed. In fact, they have begun to spiral out of control. Not only are users getting opioids through the traditional method of forged prescriptions, Mexican cartels such as Los Zetas and gangs like MS-13 (based in El Salvador, and operating throughout the United States and Canada) are manufacturing and trafficking opioids, including fentanyl, which is incredibly addictive and lethal in very tiny doses. According to the National Institute of Health's National Center for Biotechnology Information, fentanyl is about five thousand times more powerful than a same-sized dose of heroin.

While things are looking pretty optimistic in our big, highly educated cities where jobs for the people who are prepared for them are plentiful and unlikely to cause chronic lifelong pain, for those on the outside of the new economy, the future and even the present don't look anywhere near as rosy.

The death rate for every category of Americans is steadily decreasing, except for one. Middle-aged white Americans without college degrees—precisely the target market for opioid use, both legal and illegal—have seen a marked increase in their death rate. Princeton University's Anne Case and Nobel Prize winner Angus Deaton studied the phenomenon and found that although deaths by traditional causes like heart disease and cancer for that group have been greatly reduced, the death rates from suicide, drug overdoses, and alcohol have risen astronomically. They called such fates "deaths by despair" because the victims have all essentially taken their own lives, usually incrementally, because they have little to be hopeful for. Not included in the study, but probably not coincidental, is the fact that they are also the only group of Americans facing an increasing homicide rate.

In 2007, the death rate for people in that category passed that of the traditionally much higher rate for African Americans the same age and now sits at more than five times the rate of middle-aged white Americans with at least a bachelor's degree.

There just aren't enough jobs where they live, and those available tend not to pay well. And they can't afford to move to, much less compete, in the big cities. The America they knew, the one they grew up in where a man could have a job right out of high school while his wife stayed home and took care of the kids in the house they owned is long gone. Besides killing physical pain, opioids give relief—albeit temporary—for mental and emotional anguish as well.

Sometimes and increasingly, the relief from pain and suffering that opioid users seek turns out to be permanent. At the time of North America's cocaine binge in the 1980s and '90s, about 10,000 Americans died of drug overdoses per year. That number started to rise significantly in the middle 1990s, just as cocaine use started to fall off. According to The *New York Times*, deaths from opioid overdoses passed the record number of gun deaths in the United States (recorded in 1993, during the cocaine wars) in 2010, the record number of HIV-related deaths (recorded in 1995) in 2012, and even the record number of auto-related deaths (recorded in 1972) in 2014. They reported that "roughly 64,000" Americans died of opioid overdoses in 2016, a 540 percent increase over three years. That's more men and women than the United States lost in the entire Vietnam conflict. And it continues to go up.

It's a problem that won't go away as quickly as the crack epidemic did. First of all, there are far more users. Second, the awful effects are not as obvious—there aren't shambling opioid users begging in our streets or gangs shooting it over who had the right to sell fentanyl in your neighborhood (at least not yet). And finally, most importantly, the desire for opioids is unlikely to wane because the conditions that made people want them are not going away anytime soon. "Policies, even ones that successfully improve earnings and jobs, or redistribute income, will take many years to reverse the mortality and morbidity increase," the Case and Deaton study declared. "Those in midlife now are likely to do much worse in old age than those currently older than 65."

Alex is in that group. Kevin is not.

Kevin graduated from West Point and while it wasn't always smooth for him, successfully transformed himself from soldier to DEA agent to tire store owner and high school coach.

Alex did not finish his degree, never became an architect or even a teacher. His chosen profession, that of drug trafficker, is no longer viable for him, and it left him with terrible aches and pains and no short supply of regret and guilt. He is a largely uneducated middle-aged white person at the very time when being one has actually become dangerous. Florida, it should be kept in mind, ranks third in the nation in opioid overdose deaths.

It's unlikely that Alex will ever get caught up in the opioid crisis if he stays close with Kevin. No longer naïve to the signs of drug abuse, or willing to enable anyone's habit, Kevin will ensure that his old pal doesn't go down that road.

As long as they stay together, Alex will probably be fine.